The Private Letters of Countess Erzsébet Báthory

Kimberly L. Craft, Esq.

(The Author of *Infamous Lady: The True Story of Countess Erzsébet Báthory*)

The Private Letters of Countess Erzsébet Báthory
First Edition

© 2011 by Kimberly L. Craft. All rights reserved. No part of this publication may be reproduced, stored in a retrieval system, or transmitted, in any form or by any means, electronic, mechanical, photocopying, recording, or otherwise, without prior written permission.

Printed in the United States of America.

ACKNOWLEDGEMENTS

I offer my thanks first to those researchers who have already given us so much on the controversial and complex subject of Erzsébet (Elizabeth) Báthory and to whom I am most grateful: in Hungary, László Nagy, Katalin Péter, Irma Szádeczky-Kardoss and Gábor Várkonyi; in the U.K., Tony Thorne; in Germany, Michael Farin; and in the U.S., Dennis Báthory-Kitsz and the late Raymond T. McNally.

I am also deeply grateful for all of the assistance from archivists Zsófia Komlósi-Gera and Éva Horváth, as well as the director, János Kalmár, at the Hungarian National Archives (MOL) in Budapest. I would also like to thank Vicky Janik and Angela Kafcsak for their help with the translations, as well as their continued support and insight into Hungarian history and culture.

From the Community of Báthory Scholars & Enthusiasts (www.InfamousLady.com), I could not have finished this project without the constant encouragement and enthusiasm of our administrator, Liz Carrington, and friends from around the world, including: Laresa Tapia, Charles Everett, Suzann Bain, Michael Workman, Brian Rapp, François Floc'h, Dennis Báthory-Kitsz, Bec Wurzbacher, Ravin Tija Maurice, Paul Bogusz, Jason O'Keefe, Laurie Feyerer Hinderman, Rebecca Johns Trissler, Jim Haggard, James Jeffrey Paul, Peter Sproch, Tereza Viera-Reed, and Elaine Lamkin. I am also grateful for all of our members, and for those who supported my first project on the Countess, *Infamous Lady: The True Story of Countess Erzsébet Báthory*.

I hope you all enjoy this latest glimpse into Countess Báthory's life.

ABOUT THE LETTERS

There are over forty letters assembled here written by, or on behalf of, Countess Erzsébet (Elizabeth) Báthory (1560-1614). For those already familiar with Countess Báthory's biography, this book offers new source material and provides more insight into her daily life and situation. This work also serves as an important supplement to the book, *Infamous Lady: The True Story of Countess Erzsébet Báthory*. For those who are just beginning their exploration of Countess Báthory, these letters reveal a glimpse into the life of a controversial noblewoman who lived during the late 16th and early 17th centuries. A basic biographical sketch is also provided.

Of course, Countess Báthory's letters are of primary importance, many of which are published here in English for the first time. These include business notes and memos written to her accountant, András Hájas, and her castle provisor and property manager, Imre Vasváry; an urgent and private letter to her court master, Benedek Deseö; and correspondence regarding civil and criminal matters to her deputy sheriff, Balázs Kisfaludi. These letters demonstrate the depth of her administrative capabilities and meticulous concern for her property.

We also have her most private writings penned to fellow nobility: a warning letter to Lord György Bánffy who ruthlessly invaded her property; the frustrated disbelief she expresses to Lord Pál Nyáry when inexplicably denied access to her castle by the Germans in Pozsony; and, finally, the confidential letters written to her long-time friend, Count Ferenc Batthyány. These letters tell us much about her daily life and provide insight into the historical events taking place in her world. Here we find her pleas for help, asking Lord Batthyány for his advice in a time of dangerous politics and treachery. We learn of her fear when the country is invaded during a rebellion, her manor home commandeered, towns destroyed, and people killed; her depression and frustration just weeks after her husband's death; and also her unwavering obedience to duty throughout. Just months before her arrest, when she surely knew that forces were conspiring to confiscate her property and take her into custody, she still tended to her daily routines, requesting help from Batthyány for roof maintenance on their shared home in Vienna, and asking the local sheriff to inquire after two hooligans. There is no sensationalism here, no stories of torture or bloodlust told by witnesses and embellished over the years by fiction writers. We have only the words of the woman herself.

It is both ironic and telling that, while many noble families have maintained private or national archives in which letters, documents, and heirlooms are stored, no such archive exists for the Báthorys. This is particularly odd since the Báthory family included a king, cardinal, princes, counts, countesses, and an enormously wealthy dynasty that endured over four hundred years in Central and Eastern Europe. Perhaps we have simply not yet found the archive, or perhaps it has been lost to us—the victim of wars, theft, or deliberate destruction by those who hated and feared what the Báthory name later came to mean.

Equally ironic, however, is the fact that a related archive, that of Countess Báthory's husband, Ferenc (Francis) Nádasdy, exists but is shockingly small in its holdings given the enormous size of the family's wealth. Ferenc Nádasdy and his wife owned dozens of estates spread across multiple countries and, like all large landowners, communicated frequently regarding administrative, personal and political matters. Yet, only a few dozen correspondences remain. These meager holdings are held in the Nádasdy Archives of the Hungarian National Archives (Magyar Országos Levéltár). And of these, only a few are private in nature—the rest are primarily administrative memos, routine in nature, written to and from servants.

This scanty supply of resources has left researchers perplexed. Gábor Várkonyi, for example, wondered if, perhaps, a separate archive exists in some other location which houses more of the private correspondence. But if so, where?

The third irony is that the majority of currently known private letters written by Countess Báthory are found neither in

Báthory nor Nádasdy Archives but rather in the archives of the Batthyány family! Ferenc Batthyány was a family friend and military colleague of Ferenc Nádasdy. After Count Nádasdy's death, Lady Báthory wrote frequently to Batthyány for advice. Fortunately for us, the Batthyány family preserved a number of her letters which are the subject matter of this book. (Indeed, we also find that the Batthyány family preserved two letters from Ferenc Nádasdy written to neighboring lord, Miklós Pálffy!) Unfortunately, since Count Batthyány's initiating correspondence and replies are not available, we must speculate at times as to the nature of the conversation. Count Batthyány's letters were received by Countess Báthory and would have been kept amongst her private papers, many of which, as discussed, are missing.

We do know, however, that in her lifetime Lady Báthory maintained all of her family's correspondence. For example, In February of 1604, one month after her husband's death, the newly widowed Countess Báthory received a letter from Lord Batthyány, requesting that she send various documents from amongst the late Count Nádasdy's papers. The flustered widow replied that she had not yet had time to open her husband's letter chest or go through his papers. This chest and its holdings must have been significant, since she had to summon her court master, Imre Megyery, to assist her in sifting through the contents. She also apologized that she could not give Batthyány a specific date as to when the review would be completed.

We also know that she maintained her own correspondence in a personal letter chest which she kept at her disposal even in captivity. Important documents, including a copy of her will, were located here. After her death, her son Pál (Paul) retrieved her will and wrote on it (no date): "I give this letter to Mr. Megyery from the chest/box that was my mother's box for letters." It is signed, *Comes Paulus de Nadasd, manu propria* (Count Paul Nádasdy, written by my own hand). So, it is not any fault of Countess Báthory that so little of her correspondence remains today. However, we are fortunate to have at least a few of her writings preserved. As mentioned, the majority of her private letters are presently located in the Batthyány Archives of the Hungarian National Archives in Budapest. Other pieces can be found in the Nádasdy Archives and the Thurzó Archives at Bytca. We have assembled the majority of what remains and respectfully present it here to a new generation of scholars and enthusiasts. Historical background information is also provided, wherever possible, so that the reader might better understand the context of these letters.

COUNTESS BÁTHORY'S HANDWRITING

Scholars and enthusiasts have, for some time, debated over Countess Báthory's handwriting; specifically, which of the letters were penned in her hand and which were not. Like most of the nobility of her day, Erzsébet Báthory employed various servants to take dictation for her. Indeed, a review of the nearly fifty letters presented here, all of which bear some version of her signature, demonstrates a variety of handwriting styles. These documents were obviously written by a number of people, so the real question becomes: which ones did she herself pen?

Fortunately for this writer, with the ability to review so many letters and handwriting samples simultaneously, distinctions and trends appeared immediately. First, the letters can be distinguished both by handwriting style and content. Specifically, the majority of relatively unimportant, administrative-style memos are written rather simply: the cursive handwriting is almost childish—simple and crude, even "messy" and often difficult to read. Little care is given to elegance; lines of sentences slope, curve, and run together. In some cases, block letters are used in lieu of cursive handwriting. In addition, the ink is of a relatively poor quality, and fading has taken place over the years. Often, the spelling is archaic, even for the time, including errors and a lack of punctuation. This leads to the conclusion that the writer, likely a scribe, was either elderly and trained in spelling methods used over a generation prior, or better educated than most but not superbly educated. Finally, Countess Báthory's signature includes her full title of nobility in these documents, such as, "Countess Elizabeth of Bator, " or, "Her Ladyship, Erzsébet Báthory," and so forth.

And then, there is a second category of letters, quite different by comparison. These are written almost exclusively to

Ferenc Batthyány, but there is also another to her confidante, Court Master Benedek Deseö. These letters are highly personal in nature and express important information, concerns, or requests. The handwriting is stunningly elegant: clear and articulate, with magnificently straight lines (almost ruler-straight). The ink is as expensive as the parchment: over 400 years later, it is still a deep black color that has refused to fade (likely, expensive squid ink imported from Italy). The grammar and spelling are almost always error free and more "modern," obviously written by someone who has been superbly educated. These letters to Lord Batthyány were written not by an underling who dutifully penned his lady's title, but by someone who signed them—as one colleague to another—simply as, "Báthory Erzsébet (Elizabeth Báthory)." It is the opinion of this author that these letters were indeed written by Her Ladyship and in her own hand.

We are left, however, with a final mystery. In those days, the nobility could clearly indicate whether letters were written in their own hand, versus that of a scribe, by using the Latin abbreviations, *M.P.* or *manu p.p.*, or the full *manu propria* (by my own hand), which followed the signature. In the case of Countess Báthory's letters given here, not a single one is designated, *M.P.* (Note: a few letters have the symbol for "etc." after her name, in lieu of writing out her full title.) Thus, the conclusive proof is missing. On the other hand, it is likely that this nomenclature was not needed: because she corresponded so frequently with Ferenc Batthyány and other high nobles, they would have surely recognized her handwriting and signature. In addition, Countess Báthory might not have even felt the need to use the designator, given her notoriety.

A letter to Ferenc Batthyány, June 29, 1605. In the current opinion of the author, this was penned by Lady Báthory.

A NOTE ABOUT THE TRANSLATIONS

Translating 400-year-old letters is a daunting task. Translating 400-year-old letters written in Hungarian is even more daunting, even for a native speaker. First, the language has changed its spelling rules several times since Countess Báthory's day. Next, given the poor handwriting in some letters, words are barely legible, and even the clearest examples of handwriting are sometimes difficult to read. Time has also ravaged the letters, seen in the faded ink; in others, gaps and holes are found where the letter's seal, perhaps too tightly affixed or too quickly torn away, pulled away the paper. Inkblots, smudges and spelling errors (even for the time) mar some of the documents. Many letters use abbreviations, particularly for Latin expressions and dates, that are no longer well known, and some cite long-forgotten holidays and feast days. Even the style of letters of the alphabet has changed over time: for instance, what looks like a "b" to the modern reader was actually the letter "s" in Countess Báthory's time.

Worse, even after sentences undergo appropriate translation, many still contain words, phrases and expressions that are no longer understandable to the modern reader. For this, I am deeply indebted to the work by T. Attila Szabó et al., *Erdélyi Magyar Szótörténeti Tár*, which is something of a Rosetta Stone, a dictionary of archaic words, complete with modern-day spellings and/or meanings. I am also indebted to the work of Gábor Várkonyi, whose renderings of the handwriting verified my own and who shared my frustration with the illegible print, "mystery words," and missing passages.

In the end, I have done everything possible to provide the best translation—albeit not perfect—for the reader. For example, when multiple meanings are possible, I provide the alternatives, typically separated by a slash mark (/). When historical explanations of events, expressions, and words are required, I provide either parenthetical or summary material. To avoid confusion, Countess Báthory's own occasional parentheticals are indicated with brackets ([]). What is neither known nor agreed upon by scholars is indicated as "speculation" or simply with a question mark (?).

Meanwhile, what remains of uttermost importance is preserving the characteristic "voice" or "tone" of the original writer while making the text accessible to the modern reader. We have done our best here to preserve Countess Báthory's unique style that runs throughout her private letters, particularly those to Lord Batthyány.

The Hungarian language is, by nature (both then and now) very efficient. Unlike English, it does not use prepositional words and phrases, and the nominative, accusative, possessive, and dative forms are expressed simply by attaching case endings to nouns and verbs. Verbs can modify subjects directly, as in English, or attach onto the end of a sentence, as in German: the Hungarian speaker or writer literally has a choice in forming the word order of noun and verb, depending on where the desired emphasis lies. Also, there is no need, unless speaking emphatically, to indicate the gender of a referenced party. If gender is indicated, the reference may still be ambiguous, because the same Hungarian word, "ö," is used for both males and females. This forces the reader, at times, to make inferences based on context.

In Countess Báthory's time, paragraphs were generally not used to separate ideas. One might say that a letter in those days was "one giant paragraph." For that reason, they are translated here using the same format. Also, while proper names and the first words of sentences were generally capitalized, there was no hard and fast rule on this. Some writers chose to capitalize, while others did not. Sentences typically ended with a comma rather than a period, if punctuation was used at all, and hyphenated words were delineated at the discretion of the writer. Thus, it often becomes a real challenge when translating to determine where ideas and even sentences begin and end.

Finally, a perfect but literal Hungarian translation would sound "choppy" or "curt" to an English reader, as we are accustomed to using individual words for every part of speech. Thus, the challenge has been to find a way to express the original brevity and succinctness of the native language while still maintaining a natural and logical flow in English.

To that end, I have done my best. In the words of Martin Luther, a man obviously well known to Countess Báthory, I leave you with, "Here I stand. I can do no other."

INTRODUCTION AND AUTHOR'S FOREWORD

In the summer of 1605, a wealthy but now widowed and middle-aged countess wrote a series of private letters, urgent in tone, to a family friend: "By God's grace I am still alive," she confided. "The country sides are in flames…the city has been divided, fires rage across the farms…all the surrounding areas are threatened."

Invading forces were pouring through her lands, killing her people, robbing and burning farms and villages. Yet surprisingly, this was no helpless damsel. While she relayed this news, she was also rallying her troops like a seasoned general: "We fear nothing and I do not myself deny the common good.…Three companies have been raised.….Those who are still fit are being transported.…"

When this uprising against her king began, she was a loyalist, but events around her were changing quickly: "…I kept my loyalty to His Majesty. I also tried to oblige the nobility to loyalty. However, I cannot guarantee that this loyalty shall yet remain." And we learn that she spent considerable funds—nearly bankrupting her—to repel the invaders and protect her lands. Before this, her deceased husband, a national war hero, had given all in the same fight for the Kingdom of Hungary and the Holy Roman Empire; yet in her own time of need, the King of Hungary and Emperor offered nothing in return.

Indeed, five years later, King and Parliament would turn against her, attempting to confiscate her lands and imprison her, accusing her of having murdered hundreds of her own servants. Two hundred years after her death, Europeans vilified her as a monster. For many people, what little they might know of Countess Erzsébet Báthory has been reported through legends and largely fictionalized accounts of her life: that she was a vampire, a witch, and a serial killer who murdered over 600 victims, torturing and killing her servant girls and then bathing in their blood to preserve her youth. These legends have generated both horror movies and fictional tales alike, and people have been telling stories of the "Infamous Lady" or "Tigress of Cachtice" for centuries.

Such is the story of Hungarian Countess Erzsébet Báthory, one of history's more enigmatic figures. Equally hated and loved in both her own time and now, hers is a story in need of telling—and clarification.

In late 2009, I completed the book, *Infamous Lady: The True Story of Countess Erzsébet Báthory*, in which I attempted to provide a more realistic picture of Countess Báthory's life through original source documents, including letters, trial transcripts, depositions and other records from the time. I also attempted to separate the myths and legends from the truth, although I stated at the time—and continue to maintain—that ongoing research will continue to reveal new information as more documents become available through translation efforts.

To that end, after publication of *Infamous Lady* when dozens of new, private letters written by Countess Báthory became available to me through the Hungarian National Archives, I began translating this material so that they might be brought to an English-speaking audience for the first time. I had no idea what I would find. I certainly hoped to discover that elusive, smoking gun: the private letter in which the Countess admitted her guilt, perhaps penning some of the magical spells she supposedly used or even describing her murders in ghoulish detail. Maybe I would find some indication of a pathology that allegedly drove her to murder hundreds of servants, almost all of whom were young girls of middle- and junior-high school age. Perhaps I would even find details regarding the plots and conspiracies swirling against her.

And yet, ironically, the letters provided something very different and, in some ways, even more surprising. I continued to discover, in page after page of her own writings and those writings taken down by her scribes, a noblewoman concerned about the welfare of her people, trying her level best to deal with the shifting alliances and treacherous politics swirling about her, someone who conducted business and ran her estates to the best of her abilities; in short, a woman who, as I discovered previously when writing *Infamous Lady*, just did not fit the public image of a mass murderer or lunatic.

Although some readers might be hoping for a salacious diary or "tell-all" journal entry penned by the Countess, we must remember that this current, in-vogue style of "tell-all" sensationalism is a very modern—and unique—trend. In Countess Bathory's day, it was considered improper, indulgent and even decadent, especially for members of the upper class, to engage in an extensive self-examination of feelings or even what we might consider modern psychoanalysis. This European custom persisted for centuries: even Sigmund Freud found it difficult at first to build a practice, some four hundred years later! Religion also heavily influenced thought. In Lady Báthory's time, mental illness and criminal behavior could still be considered demon-influenced, and Church officials routinely presided at criminal trials searching for heretics and the demon-possessed. If someone suffered from depression, anxiety, or evil thoughts, he or she was likely to confess it to a priest rather than pen it in a diary. In addition, Countess Báthory had a very reserved and business-like public persona. While certainly in her time there were poets and people given to expressing emotions (her in-laws were good examples of this), we find instead a very direct and controlled approach in all of her writings.

Indeed, Countess Báthory's letters are often the picture of propriety for her time, stylized and refined, given to the social graces of the day. If, from her writings alone, she was guilty in any way of being unconventional, it is that she was an unusually outspoken woman. No shrinking violet or damsel in distress, Countess Báthory spoke her mind plainly and, more than once, showed confidence in a way very typical of a modern business-woman or professional. When her king failed to provide military support to protect her lands, she raised her own army. When her king refused to repay his financial debt to her, she sued the Royal Treasury. When this Catholic king threatened to take her Protestant holdings, she allied herself with other powerful Protestants. Perhaps that is what the people of her time found so disarming—that she would not be bullied, that she would not be silenced, and that she would not be treated as second class. She stood behind her own powerful family name, as well as her husband's reputation, to secure what she needed on behalf of herself and her children.

And yet the rumors and sworn testimony from her time persisted: beatings, torture, piles of dead girls buried in secret....

That said, I shall step aside and present Countess Báthory in her own words so that, once again, the reader may decide for him or herself what to make of the so-called "Infamous Lady."

Castle Csejthe, site of Countess Báthory's imprisonment

CONTENTS

	Acknowledgements	i
	About the Letters	ii
	Countess Báthory's Handwriting	vi
	A Note About the Translations	ix
	Introduction and Author's Foreword	xii
I	Who Was Countess Báthory? A Brief Biography	1
II	Life in the Time of Countess Báthory	10
III	Running the Household: Early Letters to Imre Vasváry (1582-1589)	18
IV	Letters to Ferenc Batthyány (1604-1605)	31
V	Letters from the Bocskai Uprising (1605-1607)	42
VI	Letters from 1606-1609: Estate Administration	76
VII	The Final Days: Letters and Documents from 1610	95
	Epilogue	111
	Supplement: Two Letters of Ferenc Nádasdy (1585)	112
	Appendix	117
	Bibliography	118

WHO WAS COUNTESS BÁTHORY?
A BRIEF BIOGRAPHY

Erzsébet Báthory (1560-1614)

THE PRIVATE LETTERS OF COUNTESS ERZSÉBET BÁTHORY

The following is a brief biographical excerpt taken from, *Infamous Lady: The True Story of Countess Erzsébet Báthory*. For those who are not already familiar with the Countess' life story, *Infamous Lady* is suggested as a primer. Although out of print, other good biographical sources in English include Raymond T. McNally's, *Dracula Was a Woman*, and Tony Thorne's, *Countess Dracula*.

THE EARLY YEARS

Erzsébet (Elizabeth) Báthory was born in 1560 at Nyírbátor into one of Central and Eastern Europe's oldest and most influential families. Nyírbátor served as the Báthory family seat, administrative center, and family burial site. In fact, the Báthory family owned the town from the late 1200s until 1613. Erzsébet's parents came from two separate branches of the Báthory clan—her father, György (c. 1522-1570) from the Ecsed branch, and mother, Anna (m. 1539- c. 1574) from the older Somlyó side of the family. Erzsébet had an older brother, István (1555-1605), and possibly another brother, Gábor. (Unfortunately, we have no dates of birth or death for Gábor or whether he was married or not—only his name, according to 19th century genealogist, Alexander v. Simolin—and Simolin may have confused him with a cousin by the same name.) She also had two younger sisters, Zsófia and Klara. Unfortunately, we do not know very much about her sisters, except that both Klara and Zsófia married what might be called "middle-class" noblemen. Klara married Mihály (Michael) Várdai, and Zsófia married András (Andrew) Figedy. Klara had at least two children, István (Stephen) and Borbála (Barbara).

Erzsébet was raised a Calvinist by her mother, Anna Báthory. Lady Anna Báthory belonged to the first group of high nobility who supported the Protestant Reformation in Hungary. She was a generous benefactor, even founding a Protestant school in the town of Erdöd. However, Erzsébet's uncle, István, King of Poland, was a practicing Roman Catholic, and her uncle, András, was a Catholic cardinal who, on several occasions, served as an emissary to the Pope. She ultimately married a Lutheran and raised her children in that faith. Such varied religious affiliations within a family were common during those days, as the Protestant Reformation swept through Europe.

It is often said that mental illness ran in her family, likely from inbreeding, but some of the alleged insanities—temper tantrums, swordplay in the house, or an unusual allegiance to a favorite chair—were also typical of aristocratic eccentricities. It is known that Erzsébet suffered seizures and fits of rage as a child, however, and it is said that her father did, as well. In later years, her letters described both eye and head pain that caused her problems; likely, migraines and epilepsy.

Erzsébet received an outstanding education. She was trained in the classics, mathematics, and could read and write in Hungarian, Latin, Greek, German, and even Slovak, the language of many of her servants. She also wrote in the controlled style of one trained in composition and logic.

Young Erzsébet was what we would today call a "tomboy." She demanded to be treated as well as her male relatives. She enjoyed dressing up like a boy, studying like a boy, and playing boy's games, including fencing and horsemanship. It was typical for a young girl of the nobility to become engaged in childhood and then spend her adolescence at the estate of her future in-laws. In the year 1571, the 11-year-old was engaged to 16-year-old Count Ferenc (Francis) Nádasdy de Nádasd et Fogarasföld (1555-1604). The young Count Nádasdy would go on to lead the armies of The Holy Roman Empire and Royal Hungary against Ottoman forces plaguing Central Europe at the time. Some time before the conclusion of the marriage contract in December of 1572, she left her family home at Ecsed to travel to Sárvár, the main residence and family seat of the Nádasdy family. There, she was entrusted to the care of her future mother-in-law, Countess Orsolya (Ursula) Kanizsai Nádasdy. While it is often said that Erzsébet suffered an on-going, terrible relationship with her mother-in-law, the facts do not bear this out: Orsolya Nádasdy died in the spring of 1571 when Countess Báthory was only eleven.

THE NÁDASY CHILDREN

By mid 1596, we know that Erzsébet Báthory and Ferenc Nádasdy had three living children: daughters Anna, Orsolya (nicknamed Orsika), and Katalin (Kata), and that Erzsébet was then pregnant with son András. Anna was born roughly in the year 1586, and Katalin approximately 1594. Orsika's year of birth was probably some time between that of Anna and Katalin, around 1590. In the latter half of 1596, son András was born, who died sometime before 1610. In 1598, son Pál (Paul) was also born. Some chronicles indicate that the couple had another son, albeit a lesser-known child named Miklós (Nicolas), although this cannot be confirmed at present. Records indicate that a certain Miklós Nádasdy was of the same generation as Countess Báthory's other children and that he married Countess Zsuzsanna Zrínyi (Countess Báthory's daughter married another member of the same family, Miklós Zrínyi). He might have been a cousin, however, as he was not named in the Countess' Will of 1610, and did not appear to be raised or tutored at Sárvár like the other children of Erzsébet and Ferenc Nádasdy.

ESCALATION (1604-1610)

Up until the early 1600s, Erzsébet Báthory appeared, by all accounts, to be a good wife, loving mother, and competent estate administrator. She accompanied her husband to court, raised her children with appropriate aristocratic fineries, and received the admiration of her fellow nobles: Count György Thurzó, later the Prime Minister (Palatine), remarked to one of his own daughters that she should be more like Erzsébet Báthory.

In 1601, however, ugly rumors began to circulate. Young servant girls were mysteriously dying, and the local people claimed that they were being tortured to death. A Croatian woman named Anna Darvolya had taken up residence in the Nádasdy household, and critics accused her of running a torture and execution mill, butchering girls with the Lord and Lady's knowledge. The clergy became involved, even debating whether or not to excommunicate Anna Darvolya. Ferenc Nádasdy appears to have quieted the charges but, after his death in 1604, the accusations intensified.

By the year 1605, Erzsébet Báthory surrounded herself with an intimate cohort of servants. In addition to Anna Darvolya, four others—an unusual mix of three old women and a young man—would act as the Countess' chief torturers and even execution squad. The four included: an adolescent named János Újváry, known simply as Ficzkó (a nickname meaning "fellow," "lad" or "kid"); her children's wet nurse, the elderly widow, Ilona Jó Nagy; an elderly friend of Ilona Jó, named Dorottya Szentes; and an equally elderly washerwoman named Katalin Beneczky. (In those days of shorter lifespans, an "elderly" or "old" woman meant one no longer capable of producing children; thus, these "old" women could have been as young as late-thirties or early forties.)

According to witnesses, and by their own admissions at trial, Ilona Jó, Dorottya, Katalin and Ficzkó (as well as Anna, before her death) collectively tortured and killed dozens of children—almost exclusively servants girls between the ages of 10-14—in their administrative and supervisory roles over the Lady's Staff of young seamstresses, washerwomen, and kitchen maids. Physically, little girls were easy targets for old women and a boy to harass. All of these accomplices agreed that Anna Darvolya taught them how to torture and kill these children, and all agreed under oath at trial that Countess Báthory herself took a whip, cudgel, dagger, fire iron, needle, or cutting sheers to them, as well.

Ilona Jó stated that the Countess bit out pieces of flesh from the girls, and that she also attacked them with knives and tortured them in various other ways. Dorottya agreed that Erzsébet bit the girls' faces and shoulders when she was ill and could not actually get out of the bed to beat them. We also learn how she stuck needles under their fingernails before cutting off the digits of those who tried to remove the needles.

While history has embroidered portions of the Countess' infamy such as blood bathing (a rumor begun hundreds of years after her death), she was still, however, very likely torturing and killing servant girls along with her staff—and perhaps dozens of them, according to witnesses. After her husband's death, Countess Báthory could no longer rely on his protection and reputation as a war hero to dismiss or bribe off the stories that were being told about her. In addition, the Turks were still at large threatening her properties, and she no longer held any strings over Emperor, Crown and Church without Ferenc Nádasdy. She became increasingly isolated—and watched.

Indeed, if the Emperor raised an eye over her appearance at Court while she was still in mourning, even more eyes would come to be raised in the coming years. In addition to the ugly rumors circulating about the torture and death of her sevant girls, the Countess made frequent trips to the King's Court, each time demanding that the Royal Treasury repay its enormous debt owed to her late husband. Without Ferenc' steady supply of plundered war goods or ransom fees, Erzsébet's funding dried up, and she was soon desperate. The uprising in 1605 further laid waste to many of her estates and peasantry and nearly bankrupted her. History has shown that the Crown had no intention of ever repaying her, and a successful criminal prosecution against the Lady Widow Nádasdy would justify that position.

We do know that the stress of being alone and vulnerable was catching up with the Countess. Although until the end she continued to play the *grande dame*, it does seem as though she suffered from a mental breakdown. Outside of the public eye, she no longer cared what happened, seeking to indulge herself by lashing out with a murderous rage when worried about money or imposed upon by outsiders and obligations. During this time, the tension began to mount uncontrollably. Increasing pressure was put on her both by the local pastors, and a secret inquest into her activities was ordered by the king. Staff members would later testify that the death toll in her home was as high as 200.

"Only God," one servant testified, "knows an account of all of her crimes."

THE PROCEEDINGS AGAINST THE COUNTESS

By 1610, time was running out for Countess Báthory. Ironically, the man most responsible for whether she would live or die for these crimes was not the king or emperor but, rather, her family friend, György (George) Thurzó. When Thurzó rose to the rank of Palatine (Prime Minister) in 1609, he became second in command to the king himself.

In March of 1610, anonymous complaints and rumors of Countess Báthory's torturing and killing, including now the murder of noble girls, reached both Thurzó and King Mátyás (Matthew) himself. Thurzó truly believed that Erzsébet's cousin, Gábor (Gabriel) Báthory, was stirring up a revolt against the king that would ultimately threaten the interests of Hungarian landlords like himself; Gábor Báthory would, in fact, later declare war on the king. And Erzsébet made it clear, on more than one occasion, that she supported her cousin against the king and Habsburg family. That said, there was motivation on Thurzó's part, whether personally or as Palatine of Hungary, to curtail the power of the Báthory family in the interest of the nation. As for the king, successfully prosecuting this woman meant that her vast properties would be forfeited to him and the Royal Treasury's enormous debt cancelled.

THE PRIVATE LETTERS OF COUNTESS ERZSÉBET BÁTHORY

Under orders from the king delivered on December 27, 1610, Thurzó set out from Bratislava (called Pozsony in Hungarian) on a two-day ride to the town of Csejthe (Cachtice in Slovak), where Countess Báthory was staying for the Christmas Holidays. Thurzó was accompanied by Imre Megyery, Countess Báthory's steward at Castle Sárvár and guardian of son, Pál; her two sons-in-law, Count Drugeth de Homonnay and Count Zrínyi; and an armed escort. Thurzó and his men arrived on the night of December 29th, prepared to apprehend Countess Báthory and her accomplices.

As a letter from György Thurzó to his wife details, when his men entered Csejthe Manor that night, they found the bodies of dead or dying girls strewn about, all having suffered various tortures: beatings, floggings, burnings, and stabbings. Within a few hours, additional bodies and victims would be found within the castle itself. At least 30 known witnesses—townspeople and servants of Thurzó—arrived to take part in what was clearly a long-awaited spectacle. The manor house located in town was thoroughly searched, and then the Countess was taken up the hill to Castle Csejthe, accompanied by the crowd of onlookers and armed men. The accomplices, the old women and Ficzkó, were taken in chains to Thurzó's castle at Bytca for legal proceedings against them. Three of the four were later executed.

THE FATE OF COUNTESS BÁTHORY (1611-1614)

Back at Castle Csejthe, still under house arrest, Countess Báthory embarked on a letter writing campaign to free herself. She sought the assistance of her noble friends and relatives, as well as the opportunity to testify to her own innocence. Thurzó repeatedly denied her petitions. She, in turn, accused him of not defending her honor.

Meanwhile, the king had been pressing for an interrogation of the Countess by torture and a speedy execution. Countess Báthory's family immediately pleaded with Thurzó to spare her, and after Thurzó's repeated urgings, the king finally conceded to a deal: Countess Báthory would not be put on public trial. She would be sentenced to life imprisonment and, by order of Parliament, her name never spoken again in polite society.

Countess Báthory lived in captivity for over three years, imprisoned in her Castle Csejthe. On the night of Sunday, August 21, 1614, she complained of poor circulation. She told her guard, "Look how cold my hands are!" Her attendant told her that it was nothing and that she should simply lie down. With that, she put a pillow under her legs. Some commentators say that she died at two past midnight, but a letter from Stanislav Thurzó to his cousin, György, states that she was found dead in the morning.

According to a servant of her son, Pál Nádasdy, Erzsébet was buried at the church in Csejthe on November 25, 1614. Her remains were supposedly taken back to the Báthory family estate in 1617. Where she lies today, however, is a mystery: J. Branecky reported that on July 7, 1938, the crypt at Csejthe church was opened but that the Countess' remains were not found. It is also claimed that in 1995, the Báthory family crypts at Nyírbátor were also opened but that no remains of the Countess were found at that site, either.

2

LIFE IN THE TIME OF COUNTESS BÁTHORY

For the average person, life in Europe in the late 16th and early 17th centuries was difficult. The age was marked by wars, famines, religious revolts, disease, and terrible inflation. These conditions affected both low- and high-born people.

For the commoner living in Hungary, however, life was even more challenging. In the early 1500's, the already-oppressed peasantry revolted against its landlords. The revolt was led by György Dózsa, a man-at-arms and, by some accounts, a nobleman. Dózsa and his men raided villages and towns, looted churches, and went on a killing spree of area priests and lesser nobles. These rebels were finally met on the battlefield by members of the senior nobility and their knights. One of these senior nobles was Erzsébet Báthory's uncle, István.

LIFE IN THE TIME OF COUNTESS BÁTHORY

*György Dózsa, leader of the
1514 peasant revolt*

The revolution was short-lived and disastrous for those who participated. After Hungarian nobles apprehended and brutally executed Dózsa, Judge István Werbőczy imposed a terrifying decree upon the common people of Hungary: the *Opus Tripartitum Juris Consuetudinarii Hungariae* of 1514. To paraphrase this document, as punishment for rising up against their noble lords, the peasantry would forever be chained to the land as lifelong slaves. All of their descendants would be enslaved, as well, so that they would forever know what a terrible sin they had committed against their lords. From that day forward, they would also be forced to pay tithes, forbidden to own firearms, and expected to provide fifty days of unpaid labor per year (generally one day per week, except during the Easter and Christmas holidays). They would not be allowed to travel without permission, and they could be judged—even condemned to death—by their lords. Little did the people know at that time, this system of feudal servitude would remain in place in Hungary for nearly

THE PRIVATE LETTERS OF COUNTESS ERZSÉBET BÁTHORY

350 years. While much of Europe gradually moved away from such harsh laws during the Early Modern Period and into the Age of Enlightenment, Hungary refused to abolish the practice until 1848.

Title Page of the *Opus Tripartitum Juris*

Countess Erzsébet Báthory was born in 1560 to an old and powerful family dynasty of senior nobility. Thus, she had never known a time when the people who tilled her family's soil or cultivated their harvests were free to come and go as they pleased or free to choose their own employer. On the other hand, even if her people were free, they had few options available. Only a handful of powerful families controlled all of the land and all of the opportunities in which to work and support oneself. Life beyond those lands was even more frightening: Turkish troops poured into Europe during the Ottoman Wars, clashing with Imperial troops amidst plundered villages and firestorms. The threat of being taken hostage, raped, robbed or killed was very real, even for noblemen and women. Travel was often limited, and the nobility with means maintained armed security escorts. Even if enlightened nobles wished to change the rigid feudal system, it is likely that they could not. In order to deal with the constant threat of chaos, most felt obliged to deal strictly with the common people in order to ensure an orderly society, secure a steady food supply and support the needs of a beleaguered military.

The male population was already seriously depleted by this time and, after 1570, a series of poor harvests and a period of economic inflation further worsened the overall conditions. To compensate, some of the noble families demanded that their people increase the amount of unpaid labor from one to two or even three days per week. Naturally, the peasantry grumbled, but none dared revolt again.

Rather than asking for additional unpaid days, Countess Báthory and her husband, Ferenc Nádasdy, opted to increase taxes in the form of additional money or harvest. This option was apparently not very popular either, as the peasantry of their estate at Csejthe drafted a series of formal complaints submitted to the king in Vienna. Those pleas were ignored, ultimately.

On the other hand, the good people likely had no idea what life was like for the nobility who were also subjected to heavy taxation. And at that time, the King of Hungary, to whom the nobles paid those taxes, was a very unpopular man. Years before Countess Báthory's birth, Hungary lost its capital city of Buda to the invading Turks. Without a capital or an official court, the country was vulnerable, and various power factions immediately clashed, vying for control. One of the most powerful families of the time—the Habsburgs of Germany and Austria—handily filled the power vacuum. The Habsburgs were foreigners, however. In 1536, they permitted the Hungarian people to establish a temporary capital and ceremonial royal court in the city of Pozsony (Bratislava), not far from their own center of power in Vienna. Unfortunately for Hungarians, the Habsburgs offered little else in the way of assistance, and expected a great deal in return.

Buda and Buda Castle in the Middle Ages.

In 1572, the Habsburg choice, Rudolf, was crowned King of Hungary and Croatia, and then in 1576, Holy Roman Emperor, as well. Nobles like the Nádasdy and Báthory families owed loyalty both to the Hungarian Crown and Holy Roman Empire and, thus, to Rudolf personally. Rudolf, an Austrian foreigner, held court in Vienna and, later, Prague. In other European countries, the king generally provided his nobles with military protection and support, as well as royal institutions for the benefit of the people, including hospitals, universities, libraries, and churches. But not in Hungary: nobles such as Ferenc Nádasdy and Erzsébet Báthory would have to provide all of that for the people living on their estates, at their own expense. In addition, they had to fortify their own towns and castles, raise their own armies, and pay out-of-pocket for artillery and armed knights, with little or no help from this foreign king.

Hungary was already divided into numerous counties. Each county had a governor, or *comes*, from amongst the senior nobility. Each county also held a general assembly, comprised of members of the lesser nobility. The people frequently made their direct pleas to the governor rather than to the king, and as *comes* over his home county, Ferenc Nádasdy frequently felt the pressure of appeasing both his people—and his king—while maintaining peace and stability amidst the constant reality of war.

Rudolf II, King of Hungary and Holy Roman Emperor

THE PRIVATE LETTERS OF COUNTESS ERZSÉBET BÁTHORY

Europeans also faced another serious problem at this time: a period of massive inflation. During the 16th century, in Countess Báthory's part of the world, grain prices rose 170%, while the cost of meat increased 110%. The inflation was likely triggered by increased credit transactions, the expansion of the middle class, and global trade with the New World. Further, the need to finance the Ottoman wars and hire mercenaries could no longer be financed by ordinary means and, as the demand for money increased, inflation and public debt rose.

Countess Báthory's later letters express a constant concern over money; specifically, her lack of liquid assets. Typical of the nobility of her day, she was rich in assets such as land, castles, manors, and even towns, but poor in hard currency, such as gold and silver. Most nobles, in fact, were. As we learn, she found it difficult to find cash-ready buyers for her property while, for the common people, simply making ends meet was of primary concern. In 1500, for example, a bricklayer's apprentice in Vienna earned enough in one day's wage to purchase eight pounds of beef; by 1600, it was down to five pounds.

To make matters worse, The Imperial Coinage Codes of the 16th century mandated a high precious metal content for all coins, large and small, valuable and not-so-valuable. For the various mints, this meant that less valuable coins could only be produced at a loss. To compensate, the mints deliberately debased the coins by illegally making them smaller and reducing the precious metal content in them. These debased coins were then given to profiteers who transported them to regions outside of the Imperial Code. There, they were exchanged for better coins with higher metal contents. These new coins were then returned to the mints, where they were promptly melted down and re-minted in an on-going cycle. Coupled with illegal coin scales commonly used throughout Germany and Austria at the time, such practices contributed to the hyperinflation and monetary crisis in the region.

A coin featuring Sigismund Báthory, Prince of Transylvania, from the 1590s. Note the Báthory family crest on the backside.

It is against this challenging backdrop that we now examine some of Countess Báthory's earliest known letters, dated from the period 1582-1589. Again, although considered extremely wealthy for the time, we find here that she and her husband concerned themselves with even the smallest transactions, managed their assets quite carefully, and more than once expressed concerns over their finances.

RUNNING THE HOUSEHOLD: EARLY LETTERS TO IMRE VASVÁRY (1582-1589)

The letters preserved between the years 1582-1589, written when Countess Báthory was in her twenties, give us something of an idea of what her life was like during this time. We know that her husband, Ferenc Nádasdy, was frequently away on military campaigns and that she was running the estates in his absence. Ferenc's first recorded battle took place in 1578; he was away at war nearly every year after that. These particular letters demonstrate that Erzsébet Báthory involved herself with the smallest details in the care and administration of their property. And even for a wealthy couple, money was indeed tight.

Many of her letters are written to a high-ranking staff member, Imre Vasváry, who held the position of provisor for her estates. In Countess Báthory's time, an estate provisor such as Vasváry worked in various roles as accountant, actuary, and economist, and in Mr. Vasváry's case, also oversaw the pantry,

RUNNING THE HOUSEHOLD: EARLY LETTERS TO IMRE VASVÁRY (1582-1589)

including procurement of edible provisions and all aspects of food production. We learn from these letters that servant Vasváry was also responsible for the purchase of livestock, the planting and harvesting of crops, stocking the lord and lady's pantry, delivering specialty food items for feasts and celebrations, and overseeing grain sales from the Nádasdy mills to the local populace.

In Countess Báthory's time, envelopes were not used for letters. The pages of letters were folded into quarters or trifolded with the recipient's name and address written on the blank portion of the backside. The folded letter was then sealed with wax at the creases, very much like a modern flyer is sealed and mailed today. (One can see evidence throughout here in the various photos of original letters.) On each of the following documents, Mr. Vasváry's title is given either in Latin or Hungarian as part of the address on the letter's reverse side. In Latin, his title reads: *Egregio Domino Emrico Vasvary, Provisor(y) Castri Nostro Kapu, nobis honorando* (Distinguished/ noble Lord Imre Vasvary, Provisor of our Castle Kapu, to us be honored). In old Hungarian, the notation reads: *Ez level adassek Vasvary Imrenek Kapui udvarbironak nekünk jo szolgank nak tulaidon kezelez* (This letter may be given to Imre Vasváry, court official/judge of Kapu, our good servant and property manager).

It is clear from these letters that Mr. Vasváry officiated over Countess Báthory's court at Castle Kapu (Kapu means "gate" in Hungarian). Today, this property is located in the town of Kapuvár which, itself, means "Kapu castle," or "gate castle," in the county of Győr-Moson-Sopron in northwestern Hungary. This estate was inherited from Ferenc Nádasdy's mother, and Lady Báthory visited it periodically. By 1560, Kapuvár was an established market town and, as such, had importance to her as a center of agricultural trade. In the Countess' absence, staff members such as Vasváry conducted business for her there while she directed activities through correspondence from her primary residences at Sárvár or Keresztúr. However, Mr. Vasváry likely would have also traveled to the larger estates with the family retinue, at least on occasion, and was also responsible for making deliveries to the pantry-in-residence.

In her early letters, written when Countess Báthory was still relatively young, her tone is respectful and even supportive of Mr. Vasváry. In this first letter, written at the age of 22, Countess Báthory politely refers to this servant as "Sir" or "Your Grace," most likely because he was older than her and no doubt a long-standing member of her husband's court. She also appears to have defended him in a prior correspondence:

> *Our thanks, Sir, and appreciation for the letter Your Grace didst present for us. I wrote in my letter to the man that he certainly cannot fault Your Grace. Send our letter here and get our price or the numbers on the twin calves that are available today....You may use cash for this or not. Let the merciful God keep you. Dated the 30th day of August, 1582.*
>
> *Her Ladyship, Erzsébet Báthory*

To follow are a series of invoices. These were written on behalf of Countess Báthory by various scribes and drafted between 1587 and 1589. They were sent to Imre Vasváry in his role as overseer of the Nádasdy mills. These sale orders direct Vasváry to fulfill previous agreements between Lady Báthory and her local subjects for the receipt of wheat. The ancient Roman and later medieval practice of measuring grain products in stone was still in use at this time. Most of Europe, in fact, would continue to use this system of measurement until the mid- to late 1700s. For the modern English reader, a bag of wheat measured at one stone weighed approximately 12-14 pounds.

RUNNING THE HOUSEHOLD: EARLY LETTERS TO IMRE VASVÁRY (1582-1589)

Our thanks, after which we wish to inform you that we desire to see this letter delivered/carried out without any delay. Give a stone of wheat to Benedek Balas at the mill. We have not agreed to anything more. God keep you. Done at Sárvár, April 7, 1587.

Her Ladyship, Erzsébet Báthory

Our thanks, after which we wish to inform you that we desire to see this letter delivered/carried out to all without any delay. Give a harvest measure of four stone of wheat to György Soklyossy. Let no one fault/blame Your Grace. God be with you. Done at Sárvár, the second Tuesday after Saint Ivan's Day (Midsummer Day) (July 4), 1587.

Her Ladyship, Erzsébet Báthory

Our thanks, after which we wish to inform you that we desire to see this letter delivered/carried out to all without any delay. Give Lord Imre Parnas one acre of wheat and nothing more. God keep you, Your Grace. Done at Keresztúr, Saint Francis Day (October 4), 1587.

Her Ladyship, Erzsébet Báthory

THE PRIVATE LETTERS OF COUNTESS ERZSÉBET BÁTHORY

Our thanks, after which we wish to inform you that we desire to see this letter delivered/carried out in full without any delay. Give to Peter Szalai two stone of wheat and nothing more. God keep you. Done at Keresztúr, January 12, 1589.

Lord Ferenc Nádasdy
Lady Erzsébet Báthory

Our thanks and appreciation, after which we wish to inform Your Grace that we desire to see this letter delivered/carried out in full without delay. Your Grace, give one stone of wheat, this all to Gergel. This is not optional. God keep you. Done at Sárvár, Saint Vid Evening (April 28), 1589.

Lord Ferenc Nádasdy
Lady Erzsébet Báthory

Our thanks and appreciation, after which we wish to inform Your Grace that we desire to see this letter delivered/carried out to all without any delay. Give to Miklós Buki two stone of wheat and nothing more. God keep you. Done at Keresztúr, June 22, 1589.

Lord Ferenc Nádasdy
Lady Erzsébet Báthory

RUNNING THE HOUSEHOLD: EARLY LETTERS TO IMRE VASVÁRY (1582-1589)

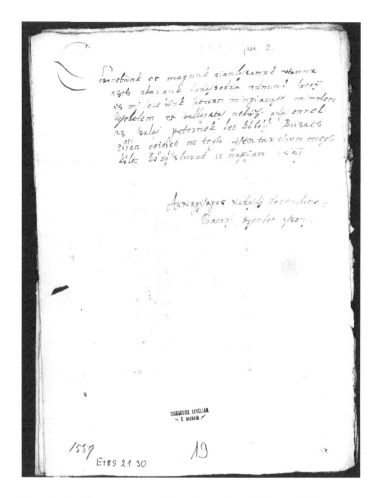

Typical sale memo to Vasváry, Dated Jan. 12, 1589.

The reader will notice that these invoices follow a formula as to how they are composed. A relatively large number of these have survived the centuries compared to other types of correspondence and records from the Nádasdy estates. It is likely that hundreds, if not thousands, of these sale orders were routinely drafted as part of the ordinary business trade between the Nádasdys and their neighboring subjects.

The handwriting on each of these notes, ranging from sophisticated penmanship to barely literate printing, differs amongst them, as well, indicating that various local clerks at the main residences at Sárvár and Keresztúr drafted them. One also notices that Lord Ferenc Nádasdy's name is added to those invoices drafted during the times when he was in residence. This typically occurred during the Christmas and Easter Holidays and at Mid-Summer when he was home from the front or his duties at court.

One also notices that the orders prescribe a fixed amount to be given and nothing further. A few invoices also comment that Mr. Vasváry will not be blamed and, indeed, protected, for upholding these orders. This suggests either that Mr. Vasváry was under considerable pressure from the locals to "throw in a bit extra," or that, in his own particular brand of generosity, was prone to giving away more than his lord and lady intended. Based on later correspondence in which Lady Báthory upbraids him for this, one would suspect the latter. On occasion, however, Countess Báthory broke with formula and added a personal note or offered a piece of advice in a sales order, such as in this particular memo:

> *Our thanks, after which we wish to inform you that we desire to see this letter delivered/carried out in full without any delay. Send, Your Grace, three wreaths with many onions. If they have none at Kapu, then do as you like with the money. God keep Your Grace. Done at Sárvár, March 9, 1588.*
>
> *Lady Erzsébet Báthory*

RUNNING THE HOUSEHOLD: EARLY LETTERS TO IMRE VASVÁRY (1582-1589)

An intriguing picture of Countess Báthory begins to emerge: she concerned herself with even the smallest transactions, directing something as trivial as the purchase of onion wreaths!

Lord and Lady Nádasdy also worked to keep peaceful relations with their subjects, as indicated by this letter of August 1589. Gergel (Gregory) Kalman, who purchased wheat from the couple a few months prior in April, is apparently angered here in a dispute over livestock, this time for the sale of lambs:

> *Letter to Imre Vasváry, August 10, 1589*
>
> *Our thanks, after which we wish to inform you that Gergel Kalman does not take well to this/does not want to take this and is complaining. Wherefore, allow Kalman to see our letter immediately because certainly in the end he will dare to leave me in peace yet and not be angered. Send this. It certainly causes no suffering to me, and I wish to protect others involved in this. May God yet keep you. From Keresztúr, 10 August, 1589.*
>
> *P.S. See from our letter that 13 lambs which belong to me are allowed /approved to pass over to him.*
>
> *Lord Ferenc Nádasdy*
> *Lady Erzsébet Báthory*

THE PRIVATE LETTERS OF COUNTESS ERZSÉBET BÁTHORY

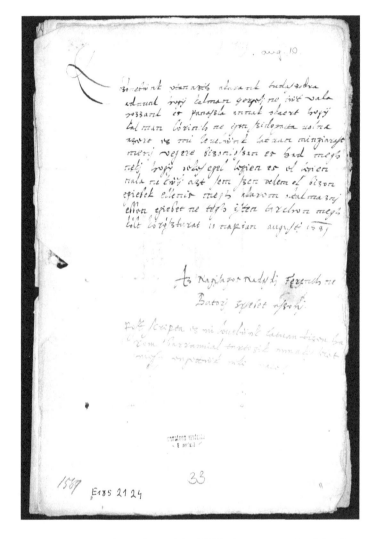

Letter to Vasváry, Aug. 10, 1589 (note simple, block-style print, likely written by a scribe)

In addition to overseeing grain sales and food purchases, we learn here that Countess Báthory also directed the purchase of livestock, including lambs, calves and pygmy cattle. In the fol-

RUNNING THE HOUSEHOLD: EARLY LETTERS TO IMRE VASVÁRY (1582-1589)

lowing note to Vasváry, when Countess Báthory says that items are brought in by her "good name," she is likely referring to a purchase made on credit or negotiable instrument rather than cash (i.e., gold or silver):

> *Our thanks and appreciation/dedication, after which, dear Lord Imre, we wish to inform Your Grace that the pygmy cattle were taken/brought in by my good name. I do not know the sex of the six but rather only the age/years. Thus, may this letter be sent/carried out. It would be better if you had the wide/broad carts delivered to the sender by which Your Grace receives delivery. God keep you, Your Grace. Done at Keresztúr, December 14, 1589.*
>
> *Lady Erzsébet Báthory*

As the years passed and she fully established her place as the lady of the house, Countess Báthory became less conciliatory in tone toward Imre Vasváry. Indeed, in her later letters she is openly critical of him. In the following letter from early 1589, for example, then 28-year-old Erzsébet Báthory is highly incensed with him over what appears to be a case of stolen cannabis.

Countess Báthory raised hemp crops. In those days, hemp was grown for food and its fibers cultivated for use in making clothing, ropes, netting, necklaces, bracelets, and even paper. Cannabis (marijuana) was also developed from hemp crops, and people then, as now, smoked or ate it for recreational and medicinal purposes. Countess Báthory's letter is unclear as to whether Imre Vasváry personally took her supply of cannabis without authorization or simply knew that it was missing. In any

THE PRIVATE LETTERS OF COUNTESS ERZSÉBET BÁTHORY

case, he apparently avoided the issue as long as possible until, by her second (or third) letter, the countess leveled an invective as well as an order for him to return it to her. While it is interesting to speculate whether Countess Báthory personally used cannabis either recreationally or medicinally, her letter does indeed prove that she maintained it in her household.

> *Our thanks, after which we wish to inform you to send a mixture of fish. You are well aware that, if God's peace brings my husband back, you will have to answer and explain what you are doing (unto). Go and get more of those that you like and send them to us. Sir, you well know that this is the second or third letter I have sent regarding the cannabis, and there is no answer. You could not account for what was taken. I am highly angered and do not wish to take issue. Accordingly, go. Get it and send it here to Sárvár. God keep you. Done at Sárvár, January 23, 1589.*
>
> *Lady Erzsébet Báthory*

By July of that same year, however, the hemp crops were apparently becoming too expensive to maintain. In the following letter, she and Lord Nádasdy advise Vasváry to add a less-expensive mixture of grain seed into the flax and hemp crops. And once again, Vasváry is upbraided for having failed to respond to previous letters. Because cash (gold and silver coinage) was in short supply, he also appears to be in trouble with his lord and lady for not making more purchases on credit (i.e., "in their good name"). Finally, the Nádasdy couple appears to be quite annoyed with how much money he has put into the hemp fields, which were obviously not a substantial cash crop:

RUNNING THE HOUSEHOLD: EARLY LETTERS TO IMRE VASVÁRY (1582-1589)

> *Our thanks and appreciation, after which we wish to inform Your Grace that already this year, I wrote two letters of which, so far, nothing has come about, nor has my good name been taken into account, Sir. Regarding the flax and hemp, if we sow grain husks in either, it will increase our yield and also produce wheat because, Sir, I have to bear/take care of your draining allotment of funds/care for hemp, profit-wise. Sow in more cottonseed, Your Grace, and in the hemp crop here, wheat. God keep you. Done at Keresztúr, July 27, 1589.*
>
> *Lord Ferenc Nádasdy*
> *Lady Erzsébet Báthory*

At the close of the year, once again Countess Báthory lashes out at Imre Vasváry. This time, Vasváry has delayed in sending a shipment of food. Although arguing in his own defense that he had been busy caring for the needs of the poor (likely a routine administrative duty) Countess Báthory is clearly not impressed. With company coming, along with the return of Count Nádasdy, she is clearly worried that there will not be enough food on hand or that the staff will not have adequate time in which to prepare it. One can also sense something of her mounting exasperation with this servant:

> *We have received your letter together with the food. Our thanks for the bustard (a game bird). We will maintain it in expectancy of my husband, but you should know, Your Grace, that these provisions should have been sent to us last week. Therefore, for next Saturday send to us all that*

you are accustomed to send, and even the provisions for the week to come or, lo, you will see our anger, for we expect guests and also my husband to return home. For tomorrow evening, send fish and crayfish. You explain/excuse yourself that you were distributing food to the poor, but we placed you in your office to administer our estates, so that we might have everything that we need for our kitchen. May God keep you. From our Keresztúr, November 5, 1589.

The reader may be interested to know that fish products in Hungary came not only from local streams, but also from Lake Balaton, the so-called "Hungarian Sea" because of its great size, and major waterways such as the Danube, Tisza, Zala, Lajta, Rába, and Dráva Rivers. Mr. Vasváry likely purchased fish products from vendors and fishmongers in towns along these waterways.

This is the last of the letters to Vasváry currently found in the Nádasdy Archives. Perhaps there were more that were destroyed or have not yet been found. Or perhaps they end here because Mr. Vasváry was nearing retirement or finally released from his duties.

LETTERS TO FERENC BATTHYÁNY
(1604-1605)

Of the little that remains to us of Countess Báthory's private letters, most were addressed to Count Ferenc Batthyány (1577-1625). Batthyány, a neighboring noble, was seventeen years her junior, which is why, in her letters, she affectionately called him "son" and often pledged to love and serve him like a mother. Batthyány was a military man, taking after his father. Bold and ambitious, he fought his first battle against the Turks in 1593, at the age of sixteen, and continued to wage war throughout the coming years. He served with Ferenc Nádasdy and, during the particularly bloody uprising of 1605, played a crucial role in the region. Countess Báthory, widowed and alone by 1604, often wrote to him for advice on both military and economic matters.

Batthyány attended the court of Rudolf II in his youth. He patronized the arts, including music and poetry and, like his father, worked to protect the rights of Protestant landowners like himself. By early 1605, perhaps earlier, he came into possession of Castle Körmend, which he officially received in recognition

THE PRIVATE LETTERS OF COUNTESS ERZSÉBET BÁTHORY

of service in 1606 and then established as one of his primary estates. In 1607, he married Eva Poppel of Lobkowicz, acquiring her family's estates at Neuhaus/Dobra, Szentgothárd, Rakicsán, and Bicske (in Fehér County). He also maintained his family's ancestral seat in Güssing in the Austrian Burgenland region, where Countess Báthory herself maintained a number of properties. Batthyány became Chamberlain, Chief Equerry, and Prefect of Sopron County. We also learn from Countess Báthory's letters that he was additionally named Lord General during the 1605 uprising.

Ferenc Batthyány and his wife,
Eva Poppel v. Lobkowicz

On January 4, 1604, Ferenc Nádasdy died from a sustained illness at the family seat at Castle Sárvár. Countess Báthory was left widowed with at least three children that we currently know of: then-teenaged daughter, Anna; Katalin, approximately ten years of age; and son Pál who had not yet turned six. In this first letter to Count Batthyány, written a little over a

LETTERS TO FERENC BATTHYÁNY (1604-1605)

month after Ferenc Nádasdy's death, we find a very different and more personal side of Erzsébet Báthory. She is alone now and obviously feeling overwhelmed by an array of administrative duties following the funeral.

The funeral was held at Sárvár almost immediately after Ferenc Nádasdy's death and, sometime afterwards, Countess Báthory left the estate. Upon her return to Sárvár in mid-February, she learned that Ferenc Batthyány had been making requests to her Sárvár steward, Imre Megyery, for certain letters from amongst the late Lord Nádasdy's papers. Evidently, Megyery was not able to comply with the request quickly enough for Count Batthyány, or perhaps Megyery was awaiting his mistress' return home to discuss the matter with her before acting. In any case, Batthyány then sent further correspondence to the Lady herself, requesting these letters directly. He apparently assumed that she already knew of the documents, likely believing that Megyery had informed her of the matter.

We learn in this reply letter, however, that she had no idea what letters he desired. One can also detect the sarcasm and frustration in her letter. She defends Megyery for not tending to the matter, explaining that he had leave to represent the family at the national assembly meeting. While she apologizes, the frustration in her tone is apparent as she justifies her own actions as well as those of her steward. (Certain spelling errors, as well as the salutations, signature, titles, and handwriting in this letter, strongly suggests that a scribe penned it. By doing this, Countess Báthory might also have sent a subtle message to Batthyány that, although he was a close friend, she was too busy and preoccupied to write to him personally.)

Letter to Ferenc Batthyány, Feb. 15, 1604

May God bless you in all your endeavors. I have received your letter in which you request certain letters of my poor husband that remain on hand.

THE PRIVATE LETTERS OF COUNTESS ERZSÉBET BÁTHORY

I write to you that Lord Megyeri is here right now determining which letters of my poor husband it is believed that you have yet seen (and) comparing (them) to the letters I intended to send to Your Grace. I will explain/provide information on this matter for Your Grace. It is indeed a true thing that I have Lord Megyeri here, but there is very little merriment here. The day before yesterday, late Friday evening after the dinner hour, I arrived here. It was so late at that time, this could not be held against me. Rather, yesterday at lunch I spoke to him about this, Your Grace. After lunch, Mr. Megyeri left from here. Lord Pál went to dinner and to bed. So little merriment here. My Lord Megyeri had not yet considered even a single letter and, finally, he had not even been summoned to me, Your Grace. Rather, court orders/duties had to be carried out/imposed, and the national assembly assumed/represented [because, Your Grace, we sent him there with our seal and he represented/spoke there for me, Your Grace]. All of the lords were coming here, and this was the reason for the oversight. Regarding my poor husband's letters, at this time, I have not reviewed any yet, nor have I even opened the letter chest yet. Seemingly, there was no urgency so great as to require me to act. However, regarding those things/personal effects or letters that I have yet to review since my arrival, I am not able to specify a time and day, Your Grace. Without too many problems, to whom God would not have given courage and (until) a touch on my head, something which has not yet been instituted in any place in nature, up until your letter arrived, I could not tell you how many or what letters I *have reviewed. Today, if I can, I shall yet look at the letters that you have requested, despite the fact that I do not know nor understand even what letters there are and cannot write/know until Your Grace yet sends to me something that names/designates. Accordingly, I certainly cannot write you with an answer. Herewith, God's good blessings upon Your Grace. Dated from our Sárvár, 15th of February, 1604.*

Sp(ectabi)lis ac Mag(nifi)ca D(omi)nis V(est)ra S(erv)t(o)ris dedittiss(ima). Elizabeta Comitissa (sic) de Bathory. (Admirable and Magnificent Lord, Your Dedicated Servant, Countess Elizabeth Bathory)

[Address: Spectabili ac Magnifico Domino Francisco de Botthyan Libera Baroni et Domino mihi Observandissimo]

For those familiar with Countess Báthory's life, Imre Megyery is a controversial figure. In her later years, Countess Báthory strongly believed that Megyery, her Sárvár steward and guardian of son, Pál, had conspired against her—at least if the words of Csejthe Pastor, János Ponikenusz, are to be believed. While, at least from this letter, there does not yet appear to be any open animosity between the two, a later correspondence indicates that some tension was building between the Countess and Megyery by early 1605.

Nicknamed, "The Red," or "The Red Breast," as Countess Báthory refers to him in a later letter, Megyery likely had red hair and perhaps a red beard, as well. The Hungarian word used is *vörös*, which specifically refers to a fair, redheaded person. Megyery was actually a relative on the Nádasdy side of the family. His mother, Lady Agatha (Ágota) Nádasdy, was a cousin of

THE PRIVATE LETTERS OF COUNTESS ERZSÉBET BÁTHORY

Ferenc' father, Támás. When Ferenc Nádasdy died, Megyery served as the Nádasdy's representative in the Hungarian Parliament at Pozsony. He continued to serve the family his entire life, even after Countess Báthory's death. Although some have questioned why he would have been named guardian over the Countess' son, Pál Nádasdy, this familial relationship, as well as his stewardship over the family seat at Sárvár, made sense.

On the other hand, Megyery was also related to other high-ranking officials, including Theodore Szirmay (Theodosius Syrmiensis), who presided over Countess Báthory's trial, and Kaspar Ordody, the Deputy Governor who assisted at the criminal trial of the Countess' servants. One wonders if he in some way employed these family connections to orchestrate the proceedings against his Lady.

He remained loyal to Pál Nádasdy for life, however, affectionately referring to his cousin as "my young brother" and continuing to serve him as chief steward after Countess Báthory's death. (The reader will note that, in those days, distant relatives and even friends affectionately referred to each other as son, mother, father, brother or sister. In old Hungarian, specific words were used for these terms, which differed from the words used to indicate an actual, biological relationship.)

In the following letter, we learn that by early 1605, Ferenc Batthyány was in possession of the estate at Körmend and serving as a liaison for the military prefecture. The Prefecture of the Grain ordered the Countess to sell to it 1,000 medium-stone weight of grain (at the medium weight, an amount of approximately 15,000 pounds) for seventy gold. The Prefecture, of which Countess Báthory refers, was a fairly autonomous, self-governing body responsible for supplying food to the military.

Countess Báthory immediately refused the order: "God knows that I cannot, because indeed it [the price] is very cheap." She went on to explain, "These days the poor serfs are doing without quite a few things, the property worth nearly nothing." And should Lord Batthyány think that she could subsidize the costs from her own wealth, she added, "I myself have few resources beside my necessary property and, even so, here am giving it away." Countess Báthory knew that she was taking a risk by refusing this order, however, and explained that her financial distress was so serious that Mr. Megyery even testified to the fact at the last assembly meeting.

One analyst, Francis Turner, calculated that a gold piece in Countess Báthory's day would have an approximate, present-day value of $36.00 U.S. To put this in perspective, a bushel of wheat weighs approximately six pounds and, for the past twenty years in the U.S., has typically sold for a price between $3.00 - $7.00 U.S. (i.e., typically less than $1.00 per pound). Thus, at a very good market price, 15,000 pounds of wheat would sell today for approximately $15,000.00. Countess Báthory was offered 70 gold for this same amount, or a little over $2,500.00 U.S. Even adjusting for four centuries of inflation at a typical commodity inflation rate of 200%, one can still see why Countess Báthory could not possibly sell so much wheat for that price.

In Count Batthyány's prior correspondence, he has apparently also inquired about two greyhounds recently in Countess Báthory's possession. One has to wonder whether he was coyly suggesting that her money problems must not be so bad if she could afford to own such expensive dogs. In any case, she immediately justified herself and blamed Megyery:

> *We further write to Your Grace about the two greyhounds that belong to me. You yet know that I bought one, but the "Red Breast," who likes his Mistress' taste, yet acquiring one sent it to me, Your Grace. God knows that I am sufficiently after him when I discovered, Your Grace, that he had yet sent it, where even so had I relished/loved it, I could not yet forgive this.*

THE PRIVATE LETTERS OF COUNTESS ERZSÉBET BÁTHORY

Finally, Count Batthyány has made a request in his prior letter for Countess Báthory to send him gold and silver skeins. For the modern reader, these were ropes or loops of very fine gold or silver strands, varying in thickness and weight but typically similar to that of common sewing thread, fishing line or thin yarn. The strands were woven into linen, silk and other materials as embroidery or embellishment for fine clothing. Because of the actual gold and silver content, these skeins could also be used as currency.

Example of a gold skein

Due to the constant warfare in Countess Báthory's time, mining suffered various reversals, and silver was in very short supply. The situation was so bad, in fact, that one piece of silver then was actually worth two pieces of gold. We find here that Countess Báthory offered to send gold skein to Count Batthyány but not silver because none was available. One wonders how much he paid her for this material or whether it was sent as a gift.

The letter concludes with a postscript and Countess Báthory's response to the Count's concern for her. By early 1605, more trouble was brewing: an uprising against King

LETTERS TO FERENC BATTHYÁNY (1604-1605)

Rudolf had begun. The military was being called up with grain provisions ordered from the Prefecture. The local situation must have become increasingly dangerous, as well, because Count Batthyány urged the Countess to protect herself with an armed security force. She no longer enjoyed her husband's military protection, after all, and continued to travel amongst her various estates over increasingly treacherous lands. Her response, however, is intriguing: she realized that she was "trying her luck" and promised to "take this road" in the future. Why she had not done so already is open to question, but it is likely that she lacked sufficient assets at that time to hire these men, as her later letters suggest.

Letter to Ferenc Batthyány, January 19, 1605

At your service, Your Grace, wishing good will to my son. I wish that God may grant you much goodness and good heath, and I, your Mistress, am always glad to be of service. From Your Grace's letter, I understand what Your Grace now writes to me that, under the command of the prefecture of the grain ("profuntra") I give to Körmend 1,000 stone of grain, half wheat and half rye, using the medium stone, for seventy gold (and yet such that/also the case that), or to Körmend medium (...) and at once the cash to grant/give....God knows that I cannot, because indeed it is very cheap. These days the poor serfs are doing without quite a few things, the property worth nearly nothing. I myself have few resources beside my necessary assets/property and, even so, here am giving it over/away. Indeed, at the Szombathely assembly concerning these matters, I sent in some of my people/men regarding the troubled estates, and I sent in/submitted Lord

THE PRIVATE LETTERS OF COUNTESS ERZSÉBET BÁTHORY

Megyeri who gave a full testimony, Your Grace. We further write to Your Grace about the two greyhounds that belong to me. He yet knows that I bought one, but the "Red Breast," who likes his Mistress' taste, yet acquiring one sent it to me, Your Grace. God knows that I am sufficiently after him when I discovered, Your Grace, that he had yet sent it, where even so had I relished/loved it, I could not yet forgive this. As for the gold price and silver items discussed—that I send Your Grace 100 skein/hank of gold and 100 skein of silver—God knows, Your Grace, about which I write that, to me, this is certainly nothing. He sees the Mistress as she was, Your Grace, [....] all that is left of my small assets. Gold, lo, I sent Your Grace of what we could, but silver verily/definitely nothing, because The Mistress well sees what remains. Presently, Madam ("Auntie") Bakacs sent something to me from the town hall. I have sent on the gold to Your Grace without currency/cash; therefore, I yet apologize, because verily there is no silver skein. Wishing you a long life, Your Grace. From our Sárvár: 19 Jan., 1605.

P.S. I understand what Your Grace writes about, that I am "trying my luck" by not keeping/retaining (armed) servants but, Your Grace, forgive me. I have every intention of taking that road, Your Grace, and to keep you informed. [Of course, since I merely profess an intention, it does not prevent Your Grace's concern.]

Körmend, referenced in Countess Báthory's letter, is an interesting place. It had been a feudal market town since the late

1300s. The castle stood on a hill, surrounded by a double moat and accessed by timber bridges. Inside, it contained a grain stock, dry mill, and common bakery. The estate changed hands over the years, but in the late 1500s when owner János Joó was accused of treason, the Royal Treasury confiscated the property. It had great military importance, however. When the Turks seized the neighboring town of Kanizsa (Kanizsai) in 1600 and threatened the road to Austria, Castle Körmend became an important stronghold for defending the region, as both castle and town were well fortified with palisades (high wooden or stone walls). As military leader for the Transdanubian region, Ferenc Batthyány settled into the fortress by early 1605 to use as a command post, although he did not technically own it yet. After the rebellion, the property was officially granted to him as a gift from the king for his services. Unfortunately for the people who lived nearby, the uprising caused great property damage and loss of life. As we shall soon see, Ferenc Batthyány's own men caused as much, if not more, damage to the region than did the rebel forces—including harm to Countess Báthory's estates.

Castle Körmend in Countess Báthory's time

LETTERS FROM THE BOCSKAI UPRISING (1605-1607)

In 1604, a terrible uprising began against the Hungarian King and Emperor, Rudolf II. The hatred and resentment against the Habsburgs had been brewing for years in neighboring Transylvania as well as Hungary, and a series of increasingly unforgiveable events finally led the people to take up arms against their Austrian rulers.

As discussed, after the Turks conquered the Hungarian capital of Buda, the Habsburgs chose Pozsony in the 1530s as Hungary's new capital because of its proximity to their home court of Vienna. They then abolished Hungary's Royal Court, took over the governance of the country and made German an official language. Hungarians were given only a ceremonial court; diplomatically, as far as other countries were concerned, Hungary ceased to exist as a nation. Foreign policy, now dictated by the Habsburgs, essentially annexed the so-called Royal Hungary to Austria. The remainder of the country was considered part of the Ottoman (Turkish) Empire. The Habsburgs then created two houses of parliament in the national assembly. nobility filled the lower house, while Church and higher no populated the upper house. Habsburg threats and bribes ensure a voting majority when needed.

Meanwhile, Habsburg troops and mercenaries were sent into Hungarian lands to staff castles and fortresses. When the king failed to pay them, these German and Austrian soldiers frequently rampaged and looted the towns. They caused more devastation to the local lands and populace than the Turks, in some cases. Indeed, in Countess Báthory's coming letters, she expressed her bewilderment that, although a loyal subject of His Majesty, His Imperial Troops nevertheless illegally commandeered her manor home, barred entry to one of her castles, and looted and burned her villages and land.

In Transylvania, the situation was equally bad. Protestant landowners were often falsely accused of being rebellious. Sentenced as traitors, they were executed and their lands confiscated by the Habsburgs. Protestant churches were also confiscated, with ministers and townspeople forced to convert to Catholicism. The Habsburgs passed laws to suppress Protestantism all across Central Europe. After 1598, Rudolf officially banned Protestantism in Vienna and began persecuting Lutherans and Calvinists throughout Austria and Hungary, as well, as part of the Catholic Counter Reformation. Protestant landowners such as Countess Báthory, who was raised a Calvinist, and her husband, Ferenc Nádasdy, a Lutheran, were threatened, despite their service to the king.

All of these injustices eventually led to a popular uprising. The man who would lead this revolt in 1604 against the Habsburgs was István Bocskai (1577-1606). Bocskai was a nobleman who served at the Transylvanian court of Countess Báthory's cousin, Prince Sigismund Báthory. Bocskai served as

ERS OF COUNTESS ERZSÉBET BÁTHORY

...ce and rose in importance, eventually ...the Habsburgs rather than the Turkish ...sylvania served as a critical buffer zone ...ritory and the remainder of Western Europe. ...vanian people were fiercely independent, however, and sided variously with both Turks and Habsburgs, depending on who suited their interests best at any given time. For the Hapsburgs, this uneasy and uncertain alliance with Transylvania required a firmer hand; however, the powerful Báthory family stood in their way of controlling the region, at least for the time being. Thus, the Habsburgs waited patiently for the right moment when a power vacuum would open and they could place a hand-appointed agent on the Transylvanian throne.

That time would arrive soon, after Prince Sigismund Báthory abdicated the throne in 1599 in favor of his cousin, András Cardinal Báthory. Bocskai had a disastrous falling out with the new Báthory prince and eventually had to flee to the Royal Court, seeking protection from the Habsburgs. The following year, the controversial András Báthory was killed by his own men, and the Transylvanian throne was again left vacant.

The Habsburgs now moved quickly, immediately installing their own prince over Transylvania, General Giorgio Basta. Basta, an Italian Roman Catholic, took his orders directly from the Holy Roman Emperor and Pope, and those orders were clear: end any alliances with the Turks, drive out Protestantism, and turn Transylvania into a Catholic country by any means. Basta eagerly launched into his new role, reigning with an iron first and dispatching legions of Imperial Troops to carry out his orders. King Rudolf boldly followed suit, attempting next to deprive Hungary of its constitution and Protestants in Austria and Hungary of their religious freedom, as well.

From his safe haven at the Habsburg Court, Bocskai watched with increasing alienation and alarm as Imperial Troops decimated the people and countryside of Transylvania. Between

LETTERS FROM THE BOCSKAI UPRISING (1605-1607)

1602 and 1605, General Basta, along with General Giacomo Belgiojoso and his men, rode throughout the region in a reign of terror, butchering the citizenry and burning towns in their efforts to enforce Catholicism.

István Bocskai had finally seen enough. He returned again to Transylvania and marshaled his forces there for an uprising. His army was comprised of disgruntled military, local shepherds and farmers, and Ottoman Turks. Bocskai launched his rebellion in 1604 with the intent of driving the Habsburgs out of Transylvania forever. And, as his men moved closer to Vienna, it was clear within a year that Bocskai likely had intentions of doing away with the Habsburgs all together.

Bocskai's rebellion moved quickly: his troops overtook the Hapsburg cities of Pest in 1604 and then Esztergom within a year. Vienna was next. Protestants in towns across the region began to take up arms by October of 1604. In that same month, Bocskai began his campaign against the Habsburgs' Imperial agents, defeating General Belgiojoso near Diószeg. Bocskai then established his headquarters in Kassa (or Kosice, in Slovakia). General Basta himself was now forced to act and moved in against Bocskai in November. The battle was incomplete: Basta managed to defeat some of Bocskai's army but could not take Kassa from the rebels; Bocskai and his army continued to remain a threat at large.

By 1605, Bocskai's men had conquered almost all of Slovakia, with the exception of Pozsony, and were moving into Austria and Moravia by the summer. While many Hungarian and Austrian nobles secretly supported Bocskai's efforts against the Habsburgs, Bocskai's own men were becoming a troubling issue, however. Many of his troops, known as Hajduks, were peasant farmers and shepherds who fought viciously. It was said that their own commandeers feared them as much as the enemy did. These men went on looting and burning sprees, pillaging villages for their own gain, and taking orders only when it suited them. By November of 1605, Slovak and Hungarian nobles who had originally sided with Bocskai actually feared his troops so much that they began peace negotiations with the Habsburgs. These nobles also feared Bocskai's Turkish allies, of whom it was believed would soon desire to keep the land they had just conquered. As we shall see, nobles such as Countess Báthory had to make a difficult decision whether or not to support Bocskai in order to protect their own lands—all the while risking a charge of treason for doing so.

In the following letter, written in the spring of 1605, the uprising was already in full swing. A noblewoman under Countess Báthory, named Zszuzsanna Vaghy, wrote a petition to Lady Báthory on behalf of her husband, Ferenc Vathay (Vatai). The Turks had taken Vathay prisoner, and his frantic wife wished to take part in a prisoner-exchange program. A woman of obvious means, she was willing to purchase a Turkish prisoner in exchange for her husband, but the program required a sponsor of substance. To that end, Countess Báthory wrote to Ferenc Batthyány for his assistance in the matter.

Letter to Ferenc Batthyány, March 9, 1605

I write, at Your Grace's service, wishing all good things for my son, my lord. I wish, also, Your Grace, that God grant you a happy and healthy life. Poor Ferenc Vathay was taken prisoner, with the hope of assistance that he be freed from captivity. His poor wife, having no other means, has beseeched us for the prisoner's release, that Your Grace would show favor and that doing good works unto God, Your Grace would release a prisoner by whom would yet liberate Ferenc

LETTERS FROM THE BOCSKAI UPRISING (1605-1607)

Vathay. I ask Your Grace to be of all good assistance to us, and take into account the issue of a prisoner release/exchange....God grant Your Grace long life and good health. Dated from our Sárvár, 9th day of March, 1605.

Wishing Your Grace good will and forever at your service.

Erzsébet Báthory

In this next letter, we find that, despite mounting chaos around her, Countess Báthory still had to tend to various administrative matters, including the filing and recording of legal deeds, titles, and inheritances:

Letter to Ferenc Batthyány, May 16, 1605

At your service, Your Grace and, from me, good wishes for my son, my lord. I wish that God may continue to grant Your Grace long life and prosperity. Lo, this afternoon, at approximately three or four o'clock, a letter arrived from Mátyás Somogy, which concerns Lord Zreny and myself. Thence, I should presently review what is written to the pious regarding a section/plot/inheritance, and in turn what is written to those who handle the recording/filing of the letter. Your Grace, I will soon be bound by this letter to be sent there. So that it may be understood from the letter what is written, I ask, in turn, that you kindly hand this letter to Lord Zreny, because it concerns him/he serves Your Grace. God grant Your Grace long

THE PRIVATE LETTERS OF COUNTESS ERZSÉBET BÁTHORY

life and good health. Dated from our Castle Kapu: 16 May, 1605.

Good wishes to our son, at Your Grace's service.

Erzsébet Báthory

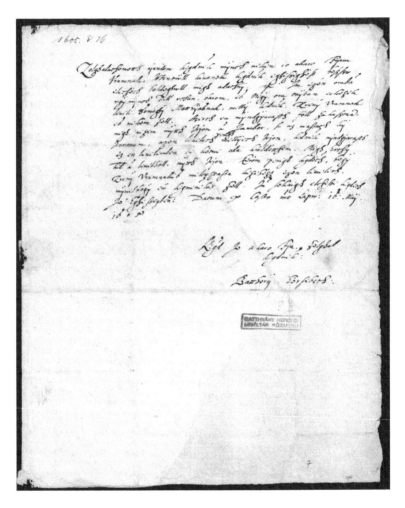

Letter to Ferenc Batthyány, May 16, 1605

LETTERS FROM THE BOCSKAI UPRISING (1605-1607)

By June of that year, the fighting had reached Countess Báthory's lands. In the following letter, we learn that she is diplomatically torn: the Catholic Habsburgs are obviously no friends of hers. On the other hand, to side with the Bocskai revolt potentially meant a charge of treason. As mentioned, with Bocskai's Hajduk and Turkish armies moving through the region, the area nobles were faced with the dilemma of showing them their support, open or tacit, in order to protect their own lands and people from attack. Countess Báthory herself also had to decide if she should send a representative to Gergel Nemeti, one of Bocskai's military leaders. Since the decision could prove to be fatal, she wrote to Batthyány for his advice. Her tone is obviously urgent:

> *Letter to Ferenc Batthyány, June 1, 1605*
>
> *Your Grace, regarding Gergel Nemeti, it must be resolved whether to send a letter and arrange a meeting. Your Grace, I ask you to show your great love and indicate what I should do in this matter and hereby authorize what you conclude for me, and I what I should do, Your Grace. Write yet in haste. I know that Your Grace wishes good for myself and all my children and would not wish any evil upon us. Your Grace, send your good answer in haste. May the Lord God protect and keep you and grant you good health this year. Dated at Levka (Leka), the First of June, 1605.*
>
> *P.S. Your Grace, I ask that you please write whether to do this or not [whether you send all or not], because I have had to do/bear everything by*

THE PRIVATE LETTERS OF COUNTESS ERZSÉBET BÁTHORY

myself. May this letter you send come. I look forward, Sir, to Your Grace's hasty reply.

Erzsébet Báthory

Castle Leka (also known as Levka, or Lockenhaus)

It is somewhat interesting to note that, during this time, Countess Báthory's brother, István Báthory, openly sided with Bocskai in the rebellion. However, the elder Count Báthory's estate was much closer to Transylvania, while his sister's properties in the west were very near to Vienna and under watchful Habsburg eyes.

Countess Báthory left her estate at Kapuvár in May and took up residency at Leka (Levka or Lockenhaus) throughout the month of June. As Bocskai's men moved through this region, raiding Hungary and Austria, area nobles and neighbors of Countess Báthory began to cut deals with the rebels in order to protect their properties and people. It soon became apparent that Imperial Troops would be of no help to them; in some cases, as we will later see, the king's men caused as much trouble to Hungarian nobles as Bocskai's rebel Hajduks and the Turks. Even

LETTERS FROM THE BOCSKAI UPRISING (1605-1607)

György Thurzó, the king's man, secured a protection letter from Bocskai. However, he warned his wife never to reveal it to anyone:

> *I have received from Bocskai the letter guaranteeing protection of my property. However, do not show this to anyone. It is only to be used in an emergency should Bocskai's army wish to enter onto our land. He has written that I have agreed to his position/authority, but that is not true. I will never accept this. I need only his protection against his army. Thus, it would be very unfortunate if other noble/respected people saw this letter. (Thurzó archive)*

Hajduk infantryman

These protection letters were not guaranteed, however. The Hajduk troops often did as they pleased, disregarding orders from commanding officers and raiding attractive properties for their own benefit. For example, in 1605, Hajduk troops burned and looted the towns of Csejthe and Bytca. Despite his secret protection letter, they still raided Thurzó's property and killed 50 of his locals in Bytca, although they did not disturb Countess Báthory's castle at Csejthe.

Bocskai and his troops, 1605

To our knowledge, Countess Báthory still remained loyal to the king throughout the uprising. She even attempted to rally her fellows to remain loyal but, in the midst of ensuing chaos, allegiances were shifting quickly. It would appear likely, however, that Batthyány advised her to maintain her open loyalty to the Crown at all costs.

Letter to Ferenc Batthyány, June 3, 1605

At your service, Your Grace, wishing all God's goodness to my son and lord, and that God grants you long life and good health....I took the good advice from your letter in which you exhorted that there are things that I do not yet face myself, nor do I not send to them. I take your good advice and admonitions over my good name, and if the Lord God declares, then shall I serve Your Grace and bring to it goodwill. I surely write that villages (outside of) Vienna are pillaged and burning. I wrote this immediately before receiving your letter, because I swear to/call upon God, that whilst by this time, I kept my loyalty to His Majesty, I also tried to oblige the nobility to loyalty. However, I cannot guarantee that this loyalty shall yet remain. Wishing you long life, Your Grace, and good health. Dated from our Levka: 3 June, 1605.

Your Grace, good will and at your service.

Erzsébet Báthory

We again find that despite the ensuing war, ordinary administrative matters still required her attention. While nearby villages were burning, the following letter was sent around this same time to András Hájas, a religious cleric who administered taxes and accounting for the Countess, addressed by her as "our pious and free citizen of Sárvár":

Letter to András Hájas at Sárvár, June 8, 1605

Good brother, András Sir, lo, I wrote to/regarding Sárvár, that I again request on the royal record that you write out the appropriate/ recommended per capita for this castle. An increase in tax has still not yet been set, but the preceding on this castle has, so far, been appropriate. Dated from our Levka, 8 June, 1605.

Countess Erzsébet Báthory

THE PRIVATE LETTERS OF COUNTESS ERZSÉBET BÁTHORY

In the next letter, also written in the month of June 1605, Countess Báthory's mounting worry and frustration are revealed in a letter to her Keresztúr Court Master, Benedek Deseö. Readers of *Infamous Lady* will be familiar with Deseö as one of the few people who witnessed the signing of her Will. He also had access to Countess Báthory's private manors and possessed intimate knowledge of her crimes against servant girls. Indeed, he was named by her accomplices, at their trial, as one who "knew the most about it" yet who never spoke of it to anyone.

Here, we get something of a glimpse into the relationship shared between them. Countess Báthory's tone is uniquely familiar with Deseö. She forgoes the niceties that she almost always uses in her letters to other servants or nobles ("Your Grace," "Good brother," and the like) and immediately gets to the point. After chastising him for not following up with her on whether he dispatched certain letters of hers "of great importance," she indicates that only he has knowledge of what she wrote in private. She also advises him to seal these documents on her behalf by hand, before sending them, indicating a high level of trust between them:

Letter to Benedek Deseö, 25 June, 1605

Sending our thanks, we wish to inform you that in the past few days since we wrote, and since I have been here at Levka, how many letters I wrote to all from here. Thus, write immediately the number of letters you sent, because you have not written anything concerning what you sent from here. If, however, nothing has been sent, I give (order) all the more that everything be sent, because if you did not send it, you know what I wrote in private, and all of my letters are of great importance. Of what type and of what was sent

LETTERS FROM THE BOCSKAI UPRISING (1605-1607)

or not, only one remains definitely in mind. We wrote it to Razkevy and the master/farmer. Tomorrow get them and respond, please. They should be sealed by hand when sent. God grant you long life. From our Levka: 25 June, 1605.

Her Ladyship, Erzsébet Báthory

Letter to Benedek Deseö, June 1605

In a letter to Ferenc Batthyány, written a few days letter, Countess Báthory's tone has become even more urgent: Sárvár itself is now threatened by invading forces. It is too dangerous for her to move from Castle Leka now, but her desire to eventually return home to Sárvár and protect the estate is clear:

THE PRIVATE LETTERS OF COUNTESS ERZSÉBET BÁTHORY

Letter to Ferenc Batthyány, June 28, 1605

At your service, Your Grace and, as for me, wishing good will for my son, my lord. I also wish God's grace upon your soul as well as much happiness. I wish to inform Your Grace that hither, you ought now to have found my letter and that, lo, in this hour, a letter arrived that the billet/camp in Tabor would be discharged from Sopron, which is the only news we hear. The issue/case is that we would return/go back to the Rába, of which I do not know what to think. I have sent the letters to Your Grace for your advice so as to understand what length I myself need keep (i.e., what steps I should take). God keep Your Grace in good health. From our Levka: 28 June, 1605.

Good wishes to our son.

P.S. Now yet as I write this letter to Your Grace, on my honor arrives again, just after that, another letter that the Lövö (a town near Sárvár) and Újkér countrysides are dying from the Tatars (also Tartars, a Turkish ethnic group), and that the situation at Sárvár is urgent. Sárvár and all the surrounding areas are indeed threatened. I do not know what will follow, that if this week they shall want my strength/protection, because we ourselves are few, the protectorate.

LETTERS FROM THE BOCSKAI UPRISING (1605-1607)

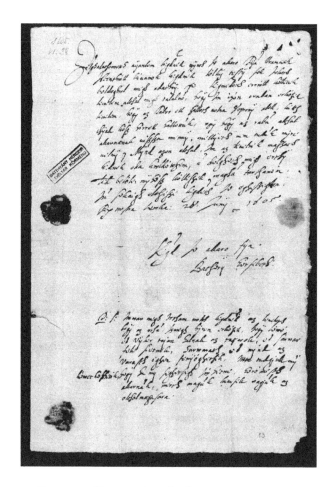

Letter to Ferenc Batthyány, June 28, 1605

The next day, she desperately wrote again to Count Batthyány, reporting more bad news from another one of her primary estates, Keresztúr. Although a loyal subject of the king by her own admission, Imperial Troops (i.e., the "Germans") nonetheless besieged her city, burned the surrounding lands and commandeered her manor home. Here, she begs Batthyány, in his military capacity, to intercede on her behalf with the king's soldiers, likely for the safe return of her property.

THE PRIVATE LETTERS OF COUNTESS ERZSÉBET BÁTHORY

She also indicates that, by God's mercy, she is "still alive." When she wrote this, the Countess was safely located at her Castle Leka, some miles away from the fighting at Keresztúr. Thus, one wonders if she was simply speaking rhetorically or if some real threat caused her to write this. We do know, however, that the entire Austrian Burgenland, of which a number of her castles, including Leka, were situated, was under attack.

Letter to Ferenc Batthyány, June 29, 1605

At your service, Your Grace, as my son and lord. I wish all God's goodness upon Your Grace. I write to Your Grace, that the Germans have come out from Sopron to my Keresztúr home. Evildoers/scum have divided the city, and the Majori (i.e., the economy of the manorial estate, such as farmland and vineyards) is destroyed/ruined/ smashed and burned out, such as the news returns, although they have taken/commandeered my manor. Why they did this deed to me, I do not know, but it proves that the Living God was merciful to me, and I am still alive. Thus, I request your good will as our son and lord that you speak on my behalf/my good will to my Lord and my Lord Lieutenant (Locumentenens) and that Your Grace also write your own support for my side to the Germans there, because certainly I do not deserve what they have done to me, His Majesty's humble faithful. May yet the Lord God keep you in good health for many years, Your Grace. From our Levka: 29 June, 1605.

Good wishes and at your service, Your Grace.

Erzsébet Báthory

LETTERS FROM THE BOCSKAI UPRISING (1605-1607)

The following day, yet another frantic letter was penned to Batthyány, this time regarding Lord Giorgio Basta, the King's own General and Imperial Lord of Transylvania: the very man whom Bocskai and his rebels were attempting to unseat from power.

Because of his ruthlessness, the common people already hated this ardent Roman Catholic, who used every method at his disposal to drive Protestantism out of Transylvania. But even his own men feared him: in 1601, Basta ordered the assassination of his ally, Transylvanian Prince Michael the Brave, only days after a shared military victory, because Basta considered him a liability.

It is unfortunate that we have no real knowledge of why Lord Basta corresponded with Countess Báthory, but the matter was obviously urgent. Faced with the burden of replying back to him, she desperately sought Batthyány's advice on what to say. As a Protestant widow facing this Catholic martinet, her fear was genuine. We might speculate on at least part of the reason for the interaction, based on her letter: Pope Paul V, recently elected in May of that year, was touring the region, encouraging the people to rally in support of the Holy Roman Empire against the Turks. In her letter, Countess Báthory reassures Batthyány that she has maintained her loyalty to the Crown and, thereby the Holy Roman Empire. Unfortunately, many of her people located in the predominantly Catholic Burgenland of Austria have refused to evacuate. She reports that, despite the danger, they remain in her castle and threatened towns as a result the Pope's visit. Basta likely accompanied the Pope, both in a ceremonial as well as protectorate capacity, and would have served as an emissary to the Papal entourage taking up residence on Countess Báthory's property.

The topic of conversation regarding Lord Basta is probably military related, as she requests that Batthyány confer with the Lord Lieutenant regarding her course of action so as to be "in agreement" with them.

THE PRIVATE LETTERS OF COUNTESS ERZSÉBET BÁTHORY

Giorgio Basta (1544-1607)

Letter to Ferenc Batthyány, June 30, 1605

At your service, Your Grace, with good wishes to our son and lord, wishing that God may grant Your Grace health, long life and happiness forever...Regarding Lord Basta, (tell) me, Your Grace, what I should write. In the letters I sent there today, Your Grace will yet understand the things of which we write about. Whereupon, Your Grace, speak to the Lord Lieutenant (Locumentenens) regarding this matter, and write to

LETTERS FROM THE BOCSKAI UPRISING (1605-1607)

tell us what action we need take, that it is our ardent desire to be in agreement with you. Command me at your service, Your Grace. May the Lord God yet grant you many years of good health. From our Levka: 30 June, 1605.

Your loving mother, at your service.

Erzsébet Báthory

P.S. Please, Your Grace, like a loving lord and son, I ask that my Lord and Lord Lieutenant carefully/diligently yet read Lord Basta's letter, which will inform Your Grace of the matter. In the fullness of my life, both myself and all of my children continue to serve Your Grace, and may it continue to be ever so. I showed my loyalty to the Crown/His Majesty, only that in the primary dwellings and my castle property, which Your Grace knows, half of the folk still remain and are yet in the town as the Pope had the opportunity/occasion to be with them, and I ought to keep you informed of this.

Whatever the issue with Basta and the Pope, Countess Báthory evidently handled it appropriately, as she does not appear to have corresponded further over the matter. The overwhelming stress of this summer had taken its toll, however. Days later, in July of 1605, Countess Báthory received more bad news: her brother, István Báthory, was dead.

Assembling a retinue, she made the journey to the Báthory family estate at Ecsed to attend the funeral. At least two female attendants died during the trip and a third sometime later at Keresztúr. When the girls' families inquired after them, they were told that the children died of typhus. Rumors shared amongst the servants—and later given to judicial authorities—

THE PRIVATE LETTERS OF COUNTESS ERZSÉBET BÁTHORY

told a different story, however: the Countess' female attendants had been tortured excessively. At least two died on the way from Ecsed. Their bodies were carried in the freight car for at least three days before being buried along the way. A third girl, a noble, survived the torture only to be killed later at Keresztúr.

Around August, the Countess was finally able to set off for her primary residence at Sárvár. By August 12th of 1605, she arrived and again wrote to Batthyány. This time, however, her newest threat was of a much more personal nature: Batthyány's own troops were now the ones causing problems, pillaging and stealing from her people.

History records that Ferenc Batthyány's troops caused a considerable amount of damage to the very area that they were supposed to be protecting. In fact, even a year after the fighting stopped, funds were still being paid out to compensate for the carnage, with the assembly continuously forced to deal with related problems. In this letter, we learn that Ferenc Batthyány has recently been promoted to the position of Lord General, and Countess Báthory coyly refers to this fact in her plea for him to restrain his troops. Batthyány's troops and servants have destroyed property and stolen cattle, horses and money from locals. The conduct of one of these men, a field hand identified as Mark Myrkoczy, has been particularly egregious. The document is damaged, unfortunately: the seal was torn away, leaving holes throughout. However, the reader can still make out enough of the content to realize the severity of the situation facing Countess Báthory:

Letter to Ferenc Batthyány, August 12, 1605

Your Grace, every good wish to my lord and son in your office/position and its fair/honorable authority upon whom many hands rely which often must be painful. Lo, I write to my Lord General, that the Germans and the poor of Köszeg have many complaints regarding the Tabor soldiers and Your Grace's servants who, my Lord, are not diminished/shrinking, but rather whose protection services/work is sorry here. Beating all across the villages and cities gallops something like a beast, going wherever it wants, who [....] if the poor man's money was taken [....] drive away and freely took/carried away [....] that at Györ the Royal/King's image has been broken [....] yet that the poor people's money [....] and someone you know or want to [....] avoid listing people whom he described, but rather that the [....] where yet for him to pay/divide a portion for him, but they [....] he freely takes away. They say that the needy/ distressed in Tabor are the ones who drive/carry it away, but I certainly do not believe that. Yesterday, (because of) one named Mark Myrkoczy, a field hand, 100 horses were missing in Csepreg, and that he had taken/driven away the poor people's cattle himself. You yourself know, Your Grace, that right now, only a mere few herds still remain of what the Turkish Tatars have pillaged/stolen, and those of the poor who remain are in misery. It adds to the difficulty that Myrkoczy carried off these cattle, as Your Grace yet discovers from my letter. Please, I thus ask Your Grace, with good will to my lord and son, saying, Lord General, do not allow, Your Grace, the poor to be newly oppressed with such impunity and laid to waste/made bare because of this waif/bastard. It is indeed true that many cattle have been taken and in just this past year, as the

THE PRIVATE LETTERS OF COUNTESS ERZSÉBET BÁTHORY

poor become more afflicted, we detect that they are becoming more resentful. Only in the Myrkoczy [....] Your Grace, let not be troubled the poor of Csepreg [....] Your Grace yet to serve as good wishes to my lord and son. I wish that God will forever keep you in good health, Your Grace. From our Castle Sárvár, 12 August, 1605.

[....] at your service, good wishes.

Erzsébet Báthory

The next day, the frustrated Countess writes again to Batthyány. Her financial problems already grave, many of her people killed and farmlands destroyed, she receives another shocking surprise. An envoy has arrived, declaring that Countess Báthory agreed to financially sponsor a contingent of foot soldiers and that payment is now due. The beleaguered widow immediately pens her objection to the Lord General, insisting that she never agreed to such a thing and that, even if she did, she has no money. She goes on to argue that the sponsorship of mercenaries is not required when one fights directly. Countess Báthory is referring to a feudal custom, still in place in her time, in which nobles had the choice of either fighting directly on behalf of a senior lord or king, supplying their own serfs in battle, or providing money to pay for mercenaries to fight on their behalf.

She is obviously furious after having lost so many of her own people. She also candidly reminds Batthyány of her deceased husband's continuous contribution to the fighting as a national war hero. We find here that she takes a firm, if not exasperated tone with the newly appointed Lord General, making it plain that she has already given enough for King and Country:

LETTERS FROM THE BOCSKAI UPRISING (1605-1607)

Letter to Ferenc Batthyány, August 13, 1605

At your service, Your Grace. As always, I wish God's good will to my son. I wish Your Grace health, long life, and happiness. Yet arrived the meek/pious servant, who expressed good will to me, and that he was an envoy, Your Grace. This envoy gave word that the pawns (foot soldiers) had been received/sponsored (by me), although I myself had not given them, such that it would now be necessary for me to act if accepted. But see that, by God, I have nothing and cannot pay for it, if accepted. These few of us left here, as only God knows, but such should be paid for (sponsored) by those who are not. For verily I swear unto God that my poor husband did not remain the lordly/proud sponsor, because it was he who spent everything, of which you well know, Your Grace. I write the truth to Your Grace that since the death of my poor husband, only 100 forints were paid, not to the corpus or income (of the estate) but rather to the servants, from the little that remains, and by God, I see nothing good in such acceptance/sponsorship. God grant Your Grace long life and good health. Dated from our Sárvár: 13th day of August, 1605.

Wishing you well, at Your Grace's service.

Erzsébet Báthory

As the military situation worsened at Sárvár, the danger increased now for Countess Báthory the longer she remained there. It is likely that daughter Anna urged her mother to seek shelter with her and her new husband, Count Miklós Zrínyi (the two were married just months prior, in April). In late August, Countess Báthory set off for her son-in-law's Castle Monyorókerék. Zrínyi had sided with Bocskai and gave his mother-in-law a letter of safe passage for her travel from Sárvár to Monyorókerék. Countess Báthory would have been accompanied by a large retinue of servants and baggage (likely, all non-essential personnel from Sárvár), and, without this letter, the caravan would have been a tempting target for Bocskai's Hajduk and Turkish troops. It read: "I have invited my mother, my noble and honorable lady, together with her servants and property, and she shall not be impeded...." (Nádasdy Archive)

Castle Monyorókerék, a Zrínyi family estate since 1557.

The Countess and her retinue arrived safely and, in early September, she sent more letters to Batthyány. We find that she also communicated regularly with remaining staff members at Sárvár, throughout the fighting. Intelligence information regard-

LETTERS FROM THE BOCSKAI UPRISING (1605-1607)

ing Bocskai's activities had recently been discovered there and, although we do not know the contents of this information, it was apparently important. Countess Báthory immediately ordered her staff to forward it for Lord Batthyány's review.

A portable vault used during war

Letter to Ferenc Batthyány, September 4, 1605

At your service, Your Grace. I wish you good will, my son, my lord. God grant Your Grace health, long life, and happiness. Your Grace, I wish to inform you that, lo, at this hour, a letter arrived from Sárvár for me regarding something that was found: letters that were discovered in the hands of Bocskai's people's army. Thereupon, at once, Your Grace, I have (ordered) these letters sent from there so that Your Grace may see and understand everything that is written. Dated from Monyorókerék (also known as Eberau; spelled Mogyorokerek in Countess Báthory's day): 4th day of September, 1605.

Wishing you well, at Your Grace's service.

Erzsébet Báthory

THE PRIVATE LETTERS OF COUNTESS ERZSÉBET BÁTHORY

In the following letter, we learn that still more intelligence was forwarded to Batthyány, the specifics of which Countess Báthory wisely opted not to discuss. She does reveal something of interest, however, when she says that, after he reads this information, she will disclose to him at once what her "honor will be." Although we cannot be certain, she may well have been referring to whether she would make an alliance with Bocskai or not. As his troops headed directly for Sárvár, it would have been logical for her to partner with him in some capacity, as other area nobles were doing. Given the content of later letters, however, it appears that Countess Báthory always maintained her loyalty to the king, despite any secret agreements she might have made with Bocskai.

Letter to Ferenc Batthyány, September 7, 1605

At your service, Your Grace. Good wishes from me to my son. I wish God's blessings upon your soul, Your Grace, and good health and happiness forever etc....Your Grace by now ought my letter to find, that lo this hour on the Feast of Saint Vacora a letter arrived from Sárvár, from whom what news is written, of which I have sent to Your Grace the same letter so that you might understand what is written. After this, what mine honor will be, Your Grace shall be informed at once. May God yet grant to you much good health this year. Dated from Mogyorokerek: 7th day of September, 1605.

Wishing you well, at Your Grace's service.

Erzsébet Báthory

LETTERS FROM THE BOCSKAI UPRISING (1605-1607)

Countess Báthory remained with her daughter and son-in-law at least through November of 1605, as the situation intensified at Sárvár and at her other properties, including Leka and Keresztúr. In the following letter, she notes that many of her people at these estates have been killed, and few are left to maintain the property or take up arms. It appears that Imperial Troops had returned the Keresztúr property to Erzsébet Báthory by this time.

Meanwhile, Bocskai's troops were moving directly toward the family seat at Sárvár now; political alliances aside, the question became how her few remaining people would stand and defend the estate. We also find from the following letter that this was no longer a war of the common people: nobility of all ranks were also joining the fight now, according to Countess Báthory, "because all of us travel in the same shoes."

Letter to Ferenc Batthyány, November 4, 1605

At your service, Your Grace, with good wishes to my lord and son and that you may be informed by this letter. I myself, sir, have never depended on the common good, but you know that in the Levka, Klastrum and Keresztúr provinces, I have absolutely no serfs. In the upper (high) countryside I have a good bit of property there, but as to what remains of it, I write to Your Grace, that there is nothing left for me to draw upon from the common good. A few yet remain at Csepreg, but they are quite miserable and diminished/disabled, and those in turn who are still caring for the property would require something in their need, all the while having to pay to keep 50 pawns (i.e., foot soldiers, likely her private security force). Those companies and drummers of the voivod

THE PRIVATE LETTERS OF COUNTESS ERZSÉBET BÁTHORY

(Transylvanian Prince) will continue to Sárvár. There are fierce folk there, honest people and weaponeers, not like the county in which, one week they (the troops) prepare/rise up, and the next week they go home, while we concern ourselves with Ikervár and other Hajduk matters. I would ready my pious servants to arms, but it is useless because the German weapons (artillery) are still raised/elevated. Those who have come/remain here have given chase. Recently, here in the Szombathely countryside, three companies have been raised, and from the Koszeg mountains they say there are 8 companies. I write to you that, at Sárvár, those from the outskirts are being transported. I do not see in anyone's heart the suggestion of a rebellion/partisanship in my town. The uprising, Sir, is surely worthy and necessary, but all are equally rising up, including all of the possessions (serfs), several gentlemen (petty lords), and the nobility. All (societal) ranks/orders are involved, because all of us travel/tread in the same shoes. God keep Your Grace in good health. Dated from Mogyorokerek: 4th day of November, 1605.

I lovingly serve Your Grace, as your mother.

Erzsébet Báthory

Sometime between November of 1605 and February of 1606, Countess Báthory left her daughter and son-in-law at Castle Monyorókerék and returned to her castle at Kapuvár. Based on a letter fragment written by the Countess' daughter, Anna, to her mother, we know that Anna and her husband, Miklós Zrínyi, both left Monyorókerék and set out for the safety of Count Zrínyi's Castle Csáktornya (Caokovec, now in Croatia), arriving there by December 22nd. ("Thank God we arrived easily," Anna reported.)

By February, Countess Báthory had successfully made her own way back to Kapuvár. We know from her early letters to Imre Vasváry that Kapuvár was a marketplace and site of the Nádasdy mill. It is possible that she returned there not only as a safe haven but also to inspect the property for damage from the war, as the troops had since moved on to the west.

She was faced with yet another problem, though. Already assaulted on all sides by Turks, Hajduks, Imperial Troops, Batthyány's marauding men, and the Church, she was now attacked by a relative. We find that the Bánffy family, also impoverished by the war, attempted at least twice to commandeer Countess Báthory's property for themselves.

In the following letter, we learn that György Bánffy has occupied a vast portion of her estate at Lindva. Her Lindva housemaster, János Csimber, immediately made the trip to Kapuvár to inform her of this. Csimber arrived on Friday night of February 3rd, and the enraged widow wasted no time, immediately taking up her pen that same evening.

As an aside for the enthusiast, the postscript to this letter has been somewhat famously translated as reading: "I know, my good lord, that you have done this thing, have occupied my small estate because you are poor, but do not think that I shall leave you to enjoy it. You will find a man in me/I will be more than a match for you." After reviewing the original letter, however, the author submits here a somewhat different reading of that famous postscript.

Letter to György Bánffy, February 3, 1606

May God grant Your Grace much goodness. Your Grace shall yet discover from my letter that, lo, today, this Friday evening, my servant, János

THE PRIVATE LETTERS OF COUNTESS ERZSÉBET BÁTHORY

Csimber, arrived who yet informed me that you have occupied a vast portion of my Lindva estate, which I do not know why you would do this deed. Thus, you will yet find, György Bánffy, that you are not aptly named Gaspar Bánffy: do not betray me with this, Sir. It is certainly the case that I will not remain quiet over this matter; I would certainly allow people, if some are not certain, to verify with the housemaster that a huge portion of this estate has been occupied. Now, I only wish to inform you, Your Grace. May God keep Your Grace in good health. Dated from our castle Kapu: 3 February, 1606.

Elizabeta Committissa de Bathor

P.S. I know well, Lord Bánffy, that this is only the new poverty, that you would be watching my small estate and do this. Not for the wealth, but yet know you this, that I will not allow myself to be dominated by men for long.

The reader will note that, in this letter, Countess Báthory makes the comment to György Bánffy, "Thus, you will yet find, György Bánffy, that you are not aptly named Gaspar Bánffy: do not betray me with this, Sir." She references Gaspar Bánffy, whose widow was notoriously conspired against and preyed upon by greedy relatives. In this statement, she makes clear that she will not be treated in the same way. In fact, she warns him that she will "not remain quiet over the matter." It is likely that Bánffy withdrew from the estate, for history records nothing further over this dispute.

In addition to seeking advice from Ferenc Batthyány, we also know that during these troubled times, Lady Báthory sought

LETTERS FROM THE BOCSKAI UPRISING (1605-1607)

counsel from Count György Thurzó. In April of that year, she penned an urgent request to Thurzó who, unbeknownst to her at the time, was away in Vienna, likely working on peace negotiations with Bocskai. Unfortunately, we know nothing of the contents of the important letters of which she speaks here:

Letter to György Thurzó, April 28, 1606

I would like Your Grace to look at these letters and bring to your attention that I have arrived, with the help of God, and am currently here in Beczkó (Beckov) now. I would gladly like to know from Your Grace your current whereabouts. I would like to call your attention to my situation. I urge you, my trusted benevolent Lord, to inform me as to where I can find you and how I might get there in order to speak with you and hear your opinion. From our Beckov, April 28, 1606.

As the Hungarian countrysides were laid to waste and nobles began turning on each other, it was also clear that the apathetic King Rudolf was becoming increasingly unstable, mentally. As his provinces burned around him, he preferred to lock himself away, spending time dabbling with the occult.

Rudolf was a reserved and secretive man. He suffered from depression and frequently secluded himself from the affairs of state, preferring to spend time with his horses, clocks, collectibles, and the science of the Renaissance Period—a blend of modern scientific practice coupled with alchemy, astrology and the occult. His courtiers whispered about his sexual dalliances with both men and women while finding it increasingly difficult to so much as secure the King's signature on important documents. Rudolf, the man crowned as both Emperor and King, lived in an idealistic world in which he imagined himself the one to unite all of Christianity under a new Crusade against the Turks. To that end, he began a campaign, later called the Long War, in 1593 to do so, and it was draining the coffers as well as the populace of Europe dry. To compensate for the expense, Rudolf's Treasury frequently sought out Hungarian and Transylvanian nobility to exploit, oppress, and accuse of wrongdoing so as to commandeer their wealth.

In an effort to finally save the Habsburg's Hungarian provinces, Rudolf's brother, Archduke Matthias (Mátyás, in Hungarian) stepped in to begin negotiations with Bocskai. György Thurzó assisted with these peace talks. A truce was called in February, while Habsburg emissaries, including Thurzó, met with Bocskai's party. On June 23, 1606, the Peace of Vienna was finally concluded. A befuddled Rudolf was literally strong-armed into accepting its terms.

This treaty guaranteed constitutional as well as religious rights for Hungarians in Transylvania and Hungary. It acknowledged Bocskai as Voivod (Prince) of Transylvania and Transylvania as an official country, and guaranteed Transylvanians the right to elect their own independent rulers. Nobles who sided with Bocskai during the rebellion were granted full pardons. In Hungary, the office of Palatine was restored, and the Lutheran and Calvinistic faiths were officially recognized. The Peace of Vienna was confirmed when a second treaty, the Peace of Zsitvatorokibéke (Zsitvatorok), was reached with the Ottoman Turks in November and concluded on December 9th of 1606.

Under this agreement, the Habsburgs would reclaim most of southern Slovakia, recently conquered by the Turks; lootings in border regions would be prohibited; and the Habsburgs would give the Ottoman Turks a sum of 200,000 thalers (approximately $7.2 million U.S. today). In addition, Hajduks and other men who fought with Bocskai were granted titles of nobility and land for their service.

LETTERS FROM THE BOCSKAI UPRISING (1605-1607)

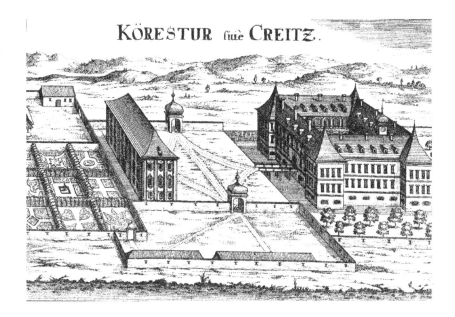

The manor home of Castle Keresztúr was seized by the Germans during the Bocskai Rebellion. Pál Nádasdy finished reconstruction on the estate in 1615.

LETTERS FROM 1606-1609: ESTATE ADMINISTRATION

Shortly after the treaty was concluded with Bocskai, Countess Báthory attempted to collect on an inheritance from her brother, István, who died in July of the previous year (1605). According to the following letter, among other properties, Count Báthory bequeathed the fortress of Devín to his sister. Castle Devín stood on a hill over the Danube River in Pozsony, the gateway to Vienna. At this point, the remaining treaty with the Turks was still a few months away from conclusion, and Countess Báthory knew that Ottoman as well as Habsburg forces coveted this property. Likely, her intent was to secure it before the Turks reached it, or before it was taken from her in the delicate negotiations that were proceeding.

Assembling a column of men to accompany her and claim this castle, Countess Báthory and her troops reached the Danube River where they were stopped at the harbor. The only way to reach Devín was by ferry. By orders of the garrison commander there, the Germans refused to ferry the Countess and her men across the river. Arguments broke out, with her troops and the ferrymen yelling insults across the river at each other. Some of her men, in fact, desired to stand and fight on the spot.

The Countess retreated, however, and took up temporary residence in the city of Pozsony. She then wrote an angry letter to relative, Pál Nyáry. The situation was delicate: these Germans were likely under orders from the king, and this standoff suggested either that he mistrusted her loyalties (her late brother, son-in-law and cousin were, after all, open champions of Bocskai), or that he desperately needed this defensive fortress. To take up arms against the king's men could once again mean a charge of treason.

On the other hand, the first treaty between Habsburgs and Hungarians had been signed, and there was no obvious reason for this action: according to Countess Báthory, the property legitimately belonged to her. At the very least, she believed she was responsible for administering it. As she stated with frustration, despite the treaty, the Germans were still mistreating Hungarians. In a moment of anger, she threatened to return to this city, this time accompanied by a massive army and Gábor Báthory.

The reader might also be interested in some insight provided on Countess Báthory's children. In this letter, she states that both of her daughters (most likely her two eldest, daughters Anna and Katalin) are doing well. She also says, however, that her "other children" are also in good health. We know that son Pál was already born by then, although still a child. By 1610, at the drafting of her will, Countess Báthory names only three children as beneficiaries: Anna, Katalin, and Pál. We know that she had other children—Orsolya and András (and possibly a son, Miklós)—but it has always been believed that Orsolya died young (before 1610, certainly), and that András was also deceased, perhaps as early as 1603. This statement reveals however, that, in addition to young Pál, at least one or more of these other children were still alive in the fall of 1606. It is unfortunate that the Countess does not say which one(s).

THE PRIVATE LETTERS OF COUNTESS ERZSÉBET BÁTHORY

Castle Devín

Letter to Pal Nyáry, October 11, 1606, from Pozsony

At your service, Your Grace, wishing our dear brother all God's goodness over your mind and body, good health to your wife and you, and love to your children, happiness forever given to you. I write to Your Grace to report on my condition/status/estate, and like the Turkish people, that I fall harder/fall again certainly enough to complain about my plight. My children, God's name be praised, all are well. Both daugh-

LETTERS FROM 1606-1609: ESTATE ADMINISTRATION

ters/girls are in good health. The/my other children are all in good health (!), thank God, and continue to serve Your Grace well as our dear/loving brother. I wish to give Your Grace understanding that once my (biological) brother (István Báthory) permanently passed Devín to us, after which in God we (buried/trotted out) our Lord Brother, one of my friends had started to occupy it. Kaptala was with me, as was Mestör with me, at the Pozsony (Bratislava) ferry/harbor, along with three wagons/carts with four servants in one, maybe more, my horsemen in front of me in sections/columns. We were told that they refused to ferry us up the Danube. The Pozsony gentlemen [....] the reason for this, I certainly do not know why they did this deed to me, although certainly by the living God, Lord [Aroloja] was not...and all have great/much...and misery, rather both/every...yet retain to summon His Majesty, and I do not know why they did this deed to me, if a small nation... Why they did this to me, with that, my castle (Zallany) was not, other than Kaptala and Mestör were with me, but the situation was that I been informed, and it was my understanding that we were to direct the administration of the castle. You might reflect on this, that we take no thanks from the covenant with the Turks, considering what the Germans have done to the Hungarian nationality, beginning to disturb/bother us, because now if they can break this (covenant) against me, then they can do it to anyone, and thus, Your Grace, I myself am giving good thought to what the future will be like, given what they have attempted to do to me in the City of Pozsony. I do not know who had the desire to

THE PRIVATE LETTERS OF COUNTESS ERZSÉBET BÁTHORY

do this, to refuse me. I still have a third yet sitting here with me, and I yet see what is desired for me to do. My servant and all of the riders have walked on foot to the hands of the Danube where there is an island there. This place is filled with/thirsty with rogues, that he would not carry me across. I am the first on the Little Danube that he refused to ferry, and on the shore arguments broke out. We saw immediately, with shouting and proclamations from the other side of the shore on the island, that they would not take us from there. I wish to inform Your Grace that if God gives me the strength, on St. Márton's Day (Nov. 11), I will go in, Your Grace, with a genuine/mighty column, and Gabor Báthory amidst us, everyone desiring justice. But before that, I wish to send in another servant, and write to Your Grace on everything (that happens). Our intention, however, was to assure you that we are (well). My daughters write to me, but they can only visit with the dear brothers by writing to them. Yet I myself am (negligent) in visiting, which is why I yet write to Your Grace. May God keep you in good health this year, Your Grace. Dated at Pozsony, 11th of October, 1606.

Good wishes to our dear brother, and at Your Grace's service.

Erzsébet Báthory

Unfortunately for Countess Báthory, she would never own or occupy this property. In her letter, she states that after István Báthory permanently passed the property at Castle Devîn

LETTERS FROM 1606-1609: ESTATE ADMINISTRATION

to her, "one of her friends had started to occupy it." Although she does not mention that person's name, it was likely a member of the Keglevic family, and probably Georg Keglevic. A Croatian noble, Georg Keglevic was Commander-in-Chief, General, and Vice-Ban of Croatia, as well as a Transylvanian baron. In an ensuing legal dispute, the Keglevic family claimed that István Báthory had actually given the castle to them. Countess Báthory strongly disagreed. The matter was litigated and, in 1609, the king declared that the Keglevics were the rightful owners. Historically, scholars have always thought that Istvan Báthory himself declared the Keglevics to be the true owners; if Countess Báthory is telling the truth in this letter, then we find a contradiction and perhaps an unfair advantage taken over the widow to wrest this bequest from her. On the other hand, she herself might have been attempting to take possession without authorization. Whatever the case, the Keglevics had already pawned the property for 40,000 gulders to the Palocsai family when the king's confirmation arrived. Lacking the funds to redeem it, Castle Devín then passed to the Palocsais.

Meanwhile, although the Bocskai Revolt and Rudolf's Long War would soon be at an end, the fighting continued sporadically. At the highest levels of power, the situation was becoming even more heated. Still seething over the treaties forged against his wishes, Rudolf waited for the right time to strike back against his brother, Archduke Mátyás. As fate would have it, he did not have to wait very long. In late December of 1606, news reached the King's Court that István Bocskai was dead, apparently the victim of a plot by his own chancellor to poison him. With that, Rudolf immediately began nullifying all of the laws that he had so grudgingly accepted at the Peace Treaty of Vienna in 1606.

Bewildered Hungarian nobles turned to Mátyás for assistance. In so many words, he advised them to conduct business

THE PRIVATE LETTERS OF COUNTESS ERZSÉBET BÁTHORY

as usual. At this point, Rudolf could barely remember from day to day what he had decreed the prior week. Meanwhile, Mátyás worked behind the scenes with the nobility to secure their confidence. He was planning a coup and needed their assistance. The situation was grave: rumors coming from the King's Court intimated that the belligerent and increasingly unstable Rudolf was now planning to launch a new war against the Turks.

Armed with 15,000 men, Mátyás moved into Moravia where he easily overtook Rudolf. The stunned king eventually ceded the Hungarian, Moravian and Bohemian crowns to his younger brother. The nobility summarily named Mátyás King of Hungary in 1608, and in that same year, Erzsébet Báthory's 19-year-old cousin, Gábor, took over the Transylvanian throne by his own military seizure of power.

For those familiar with Countess Báthory's litigation against the Royal Treasury, the following information should prove interesting. During his reign, Rudolf borrowed considerable funds from Ferenc Nádasdy. At Count Nádasdy's death, Countess Báthory attempted to collect on these loans made to the Treasury. Each time, she was refused, given various excuses why the Royal Treasury did not have the funds to pay her but always assured that it would do so at a later date. We know that she continued to litigate unsuccessfully against the Crown for years, that money problems plagued her, and that she was eventually forced to sell some of her properties to make ends meet. Ironically, the supposedly cash-strapped Royal Treasury purchased one of these properties in 1607—her Castle at Theben. It is also interesting to note that Countess Báthory continued to pay taxes each year to the Royal Treasury and that the king either did not consider—or, in fact, refused—the option of writing off her tax debt in exchange for his own outstanding obligations to the Widow Nádasdy.

The Crown owed Countess Báthory a little less than 18,000 gulden. Somewhat galling, however, is the fact that when Rudolf died in January of 1612, he actually left behind an

LETTERS FROM 1606-1609: ESTATE ADMINISTRATION

enormous sum in the Royal Treasury: 17 million gold pieces (an amount worth over $600 million U.S. today), largely collected from confiscated Hungarian estates. We do not know if Countess Báthory was ever made aware of this fact, but it is quite likely that, had she known, she would have been enraged.

King Mátyás (Matthias II) of Hungary and Holy Roman Emperor (1557-1619)

According to the correspondence found from the period of late 1606 through 1609, Countess Báthory returned to the or-

THE PRIVATE LETTERS OF COUNTESS ERZSÉBET BÁTHORY

dinary administration of her estates, repairing her property after the war, and tending to the business of running her counties. We find, as always, that she was intimately involved in all levels of administration, from the election of local officials to the appointment of church officers.

For example, in 1606, György Thurzó intended to appoint a clergyman named Peter Kálli as superior over the diocese of Csorna. In her reply letter to Thurzó, we learn that, for whatever reason, Countess Báthory had no intention of carrying out Thurzó's wishes—whether for her own personal reasons or because of previous arrangements made with neighboring nobles. Artfully diplomatic, she deftly deferred the choice away from Thurzó and back to herself:

Letter to György Thurzó, November 11, 1606

I have received the letter from Your Grace and understand from what you wrote regarding Peter Kálli, such that I might give him the abbacy/provost/diocese of Csorna. I can only write to you that I would like to do this with great joy and, in fact, have already visited with some close nobles, such as my lord [Octavio]/as my lord also has [been petitioned] by the Octave court to discuss this situation, although I still have not yet decided the matter. I shall write to these trusted lords and ask them to convene with me to discuss the matter further and offer what advice they have to give. What decision these gentlemen decide to take, I will follow. I shall immediately inform Your Grace with an answer, because you are also involved in the matter, so that you can give a certain/definite answer to our close friend to say what he has been promised. I serve you

LETTERS FROM 1606-1609: ESTATE ADMINISTRATION

with love as my brother. From our Keresztúr, 11 November, 1606.

In the spring of the following year, another member of the troublesome Bánffy family, Christoph, unlawfully took possession of Nempti Castle. The Turks still occupied Nempti, a Croatian town, and prisoners were often taken there. The situation was somewhat complicated diplomatically since Bánff cleverly engaged the services of the local Turkish Pasha to assist him. Countess Báthory is concerned about staging an attack against him and the local Turks, since a covenant was not signed with them during the war (she is perhaps speaking of the protection agreements between Hungarian nobles and Bocskai's men, including the Turks). Thus, she seeks Batthyány's advice on how to proceed against Bánffy:

Letter to Ferenc Batthyány, March 14, 1607

At your service, Your Grace, sending all good wishes to my Lord and Son. I wish God's blessings for a sound body, good health and happiness and continue to inform Your Grace as a woman who loves you like a mother forever. Therefore ought Your Grace to receive my letter such that I may inform you that Lord Christoph Bánffy has taken possession of Nempti Castle. As for the reason behind this deed, Your Grace, we understand nothing about it. In addition, Your Grace should know that this is not merely about him at Nempti Castle but rather that the entire common brethren (public/kinship) are concerned, and the national assembly meeting (Diet) is already at hand, which does not seem to bother him, Your Grace. I have learned of this from Your Grace's servant, as well as the servant of Lady Popel (i.e., Batthyány's wife, Lady Poppel)...and there is nothing to indicate that (this information) is not credible. Your Grace, I think that neither kinship nor good neighborliness motivated this action. Thus, Your Grace, with all good wishes to my Lord and Son, I lovingly request that you advise and give understanding as to what should result from these deeds, because we had not entered into a covenant during the war. Indeed, it (i.e., the violence) is starting again, because I hear that Pasha Kanisai (Kaniszai) believed help was needed, and he had launched (an assault), together both of them battering at the bottom of the Eördögh wells until they gained access, although they certainly could not have taken it, as the matter came out. This is certainly not a situation such that he should have called out the Turks. Rather, Your Grace (is) now (concerned with) the national assembly, where I know that in that case you have yet more important matters, it is true. Because of this, therefore, I request that Your Grace write and inform me as to what I should do regarding these deeds. God grant Your Grace long life and good health. Dated from our Sötör, March 14, 1607.

In service to your Grace as your mother.

Erzsébet Báthory

We have no records, unfortunately, of how this matter concluded, but it likely resolved in Countess Báthory's favor since it was discussed no further in later correspondence.

By late 1607, the political and economic situation had finally stabilized in the region sufficiently for György Thurzó to prepare for the wedding of his daughter, Judit, at his magnificent wedding pavilion at Castle Bytca. Through a scribe, Countess Báthory sent off this brief communiqué:

> *Erzsébet Báthory relates that she safely reached Csejthe, last Tuesday (13th of November). If God grants her good health, she will comply with Thurzó's wish to attend the wedding of his child. It is her pleasure to serve him. Csejthe, November 16, 1607.*

One senses that her relationship with Thurzó had already started to cool by this time, given the informality and brevity of her *RSVP* for what was certainly an important social event. It is likely that the strain of attending this event caused Countess Báthory to again lash out in a murderous rage against her attendants. On the way home from the wedding in the frigid early winter, witnesses recounted that one of her young attendants attempted to escape from the coach. The girl was captured and, as punishment, taken to the nearby town of Predmier where she was stripped naked in the bitter cold. She was then forced to stand up to her neck in an icy river while water was repeatedly doused over her head. She soon died of exposure.

The following year, in 1608, Countess Báthory was back to running her estates in an orderly manner and concerned now with the coming county elections. In Hungary at the time, the country was divided into numerous counties, each headed by a *comes* (governor) from amongst the senior aristocracy. This was a hereditary position. Until his death, Count Ferenc Nádasdy was the *comes* over the county seat where his primary residences were located. Countess Báthory then assumed these duties on behalf of their young son, Pál, until he reached the age of majority which, in those days for this particular position, was twelve years of age.

County assemblies were comprised of lesser nobles, free men who were not tied to the land but still owed or offered service to an older and wealthier family. In those days, approximately 9,000 families had already received a title of nobility and certain tax exemptions in exchange for their faithful service. Family names ending in "y" or "i" indicated a noble rank, although many were not wealthy. Senior nobility jokingly referred to these "honorary nobles" as the "lord of seven apple trees," or the "master of six pigs." Court master Benedek Deseö was such an example. Before the age of 20, Countess Báthory's cousin, Sigismund Báthory, granted him a title of nobility, and records indicate that a man of the same name also received a title from István Bocskai after the war. Deseö then worked for the Báthory and Nádasdy families until the age of fifty.

In the following two letters written in March of 1608, we find, first, that Countess Báthory endorses her choice of a man named Erten to assume the recently vacant position of Vasvár Sheriff. In the second document, she advises Batthyány on certain rumors of political maneuvering. Although we have little context for what she means, it might have had something to do with money owed to locals for the damage caused by Batthyány's troops in the previous military campaigns. It is also interesting to note that, for local positions, something akin to a democratic process took place in which vacancies were posted and positions filled by election rather than appointment:

Letter to Ferenc Batthyány, March 22, 1608

At your service, Your Grace, sending good will to my lord and son. May God continue to grant Your Grace health and happiness....I only wish to inform you that, whereas it is now time for the Vasvar

LETTERS FROM 1606-1609: ESTATE ADMINISTRATION

County General Assembly meeting, Lord István Keserü, the county sheriff and also in turn (bail) Lieutenant, will be leaving office, of whom I am aware that Your Grace knew well. As a result, one of the other gentlemen, a certain Erten, has volunteered to serve, at your good pleasure, and we would desire to have Erten who will instead/likely be chosen today. I am aware that the assembly properly announced the vacancy as required to do, and served Your Grace's command with love. May God continue to grant Your Grace much good health. From our Keresztúr: 22 March, 1608. At Your Grace's service.

Erzsébet Báthory

Letter to Ferenc Batthyány, March 27, 1608

At your service, Your Grace, sending good wishes to my lord and son. May God continue to grant Your Grace health and happiness. As Mistress, I want you to understand what I write in my letter to Your Grace, that what we write comes not only from me but also from several lords and responsible friends, who have fair hands (i.e., nothing to gain). We have found, through a private conversation, gossip/small talk, that a general assembly has been ordered, such to be done on the 21st day of April, and that the bailiff, Viczi, has now been ordered to announce/advertise it. I consider, however, that this meeting should not go on more than three days, but rather that Veg would be selected. As we, however, have received the money and used it, I know that the lords *will be looked after and can come to Your Grace. One thing is certain, however, and that is that I write to you but choose not to document it. Rather this letter, along with the lords, makes abundant answer to you what is on my mind. It is not documented inasmuch as several more have been written to Your Grace for such this thing of which I gave knowledge to Your Grace in my letter. May God continue to grant Your Grace much happiness and good health. From our Keresztúr: 27 March, 1608. At Your Grace's service.*

Erzsébet Báthory

P.S. If anything was written, Your Grace, that provides information, please write your answer.

On November 19, 1608, Mátyás II was crowned King of Hungary and Croatia. The ceremony was held in Poszony, and Countess Bathory attended with a retinue. Typical of a stressful social event, servants claimed that her attendants were brutally tortured during the trip, this time with molten iron. According to accounts, the girls were sent back to Keresztúr barely alive, where some died shortly thereafter.

LETTERS FROM 1606-1609: ESTATE ADMINISTRATION

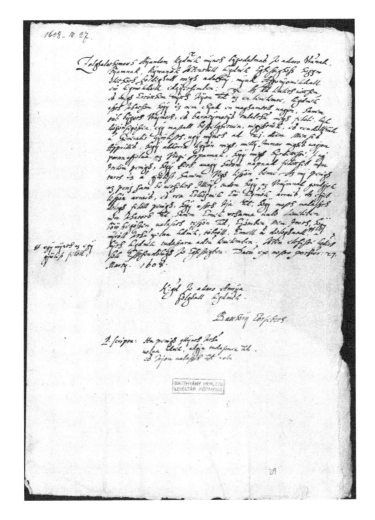

Letter to Ferenc Batthyány, March 27, 1608.

In early 1609, Countess Báthory sent a letter to Balázs Kisfaludi (Kysfaludi), the Deputy Sheriff of Vas County. In her position, she was responsible for the administration of civil as well as criminal justice on her estates, including, as we shall see, even relatively minor matters. In the first case, an old woman's

THE PRIVATE LETTERS OF COUNTESS ERZSÉBET BÁTHORY

home in the town of Tokorcs has been vandalized and her property stolen on several occasions by locals. Her daughter was also raped. The woman petitioned Lady Báthory for help, who then forwarded the case to Kisfaludi. Although the letter has been damaged and parts are impossible to make out, enough is available to indicate that Countess Báthory desired punishment for the wrongdoers. Again, one cannot help wonder at the apparent contradiction. The woman believed to privately torture and murder young servant girls, some of whom came from the nobility, was here demanding justice now for an old woman of relatively no account and a questionable background:

Letter to Balázs Kisfaludi, Jan. 19, 1609

May God grant you many blessings, Your Grace. You shall discover from our letter the reason behind certain recent activities, such that Your Grace pursues the matter. We bring this matter to you on behalf of the "known madam" of Tokorcs who has petitioned us and in whose house this matter/incident took place. The news reached us that the abode [....] of one Menyecske [....] in which house had been reared since childhood, which Menyecske now had Nehezke and asked him to confess, of which Nehezke confessed to three incidents/parts, having taken in turn from the miserable old woman. Since then/such that Vej the brother/buddy as a servant, immediately began to confess. Now also involved in the three incidents and implicated was István Dül who came out of the house, that he some cattle/chattel taken (up to Dulny)...as much at fault. This I ask you, that if they go out, you would yet command that the poor old lady's cattle/chattel not be pil-

laged/pilfered, where she has faulted no one; rather, the ones who are at fault should be punished. God grant you happiness, Your Grace. From our Sárvár, 19 January, 1609.

Elizabetha Comitissa de Bathor

In the next letter to Kisfaludi, written that same year, Countess Báthory concerns herself with the appropriate legal suretyship required for two young dental apprentices, Mathi and Peter Magaszy. We find here that Countess Báthory is well versed in the law. In those days, young boys entering a guild or brotherhood as apprentices generally required a bond, guarantor or suretyship (essentially insurance or sponsorship on their behalf) before they were accepted. A certain Lord István Lampert had previously claimed that the guarantors would take full responsibility for the boys, but Countess Báthory is not satisfied. Appropriate paperwork was not delivered, and an ordinary suretyship would not be sufficient for minor children. However, she asks Kisfaludi to look into the law and see how it applies to these boys:

Letter to Blazius Kysfaludi, 19 March, 1609

May God continue to grant you much goodness, Your Grace. By now ought Your Grace to have received our letter that we came to bring to Your Grace, as the magisterial judge over servants. Lord István Lampert, the sole witness for the noble lads in dentistry, corresponds that the guarantors would be responsible for the minors, Mathi Magaszy and Peter Magaszy. Therein for us there is no doubt that this was not delivered and that the suretyship does not guarantee minors. But the Statute (Procotokemot) has been sent for, and still needs to be read into and gathered by those who tender the law if it is found under the law of the Concordance. However, it should provide the answer and apply to the two of them here. Also, the law should be valid for six months. Thus go, Your Grace. Inform us as to the evidence in a letter that we shall expect from you. God grant you long life and good health. Dated from our Sárvár: 19 March, 1609.

*G[enerose] E[gregia] D[omina] V[est]ra
In omnibus benevola (in all things wishing well)*

Countess Erzsébet Báthory

Woodcut of a dentist at work, 1568

7

THE FINAL DAYS: LETTERS AND DOCUMENTS FROM 1610 (INCLUDING EPILOGUE AND SUPPLEMENT)

As those familiar with the story of the Countess know, by 1610, the rumors that she was torturing and murdering her young servant girls had spread not only amongst her people but also to the highest authority, including King Mátyás. An inquest began in earnest: the king's officials began interrogating locals, servants, and minor nobility under oath, searching for evidence against Countess Báthory. For readers interested in the complete details, including the legal proceedings, witness statements, trial documents, and official letters, the details are provided in *Infamous Lady: The True Story of Countess Erzsébet Báthory*. Here, however, we contrast the legal and political intrigue swirling about her with the Countess' own letters from the period.

THE PRIVATE LETTERS OF COUNTESS ERZSÉBET BÁTHORY

Despite the proceedings beginning against her, Erzsébet Báthory continued to tend to the ordinary, even mundane, administration of her estates. In this letter from June of 1610, six months before her arrest, for example, she writes to inform Ferenc Batthyány that the roof of their shared home in Vienna needs repairs (unfortunately, certain parts are illegible):

Letter to Ferenc Batthyány, June 28, 1610

At your service, Your Grace. I wish all goodness upon my son and lord, and may God grant you much goodness. Since having viewed the roof of the Vienna home and being told that if it remains in this state in the coming years that everything will be lost, at great expense to rebuild it, I will inquire further. Right now, I wish to begin repairs. As to how much completion will cost, it was said that 273 Renissel (?) are needed for the improvements. [All there send Ausczugi... something else for me:] I remember how, through the good will of my poor husband between us, you had (hath you) the upper house in that part of the building, when we brought you help. Wherefore, I request of Your Grace, to consult with you completely and to ask if you would help with the construction because of its great cost. [If, in turn, Your Grace would not like to do this, then I ask please do not try to cause harm both for me and all my children, (to demand that) because of such reasons that all of the roof defects be fixed.] All of the house rent/income of 100 forints per year went to the cost of construction, and also the money on hand can give (you) yet the house wages/rent. (Always used by Your Grace and your pious servants to whom the letter thou), not be

THE FINAL DAYS: LETTERS AND DOCUMENTS FROM 1610 (INCLUDING EPILOGUE AND SUPPLEMENT)

clandestine, only from this was yet discovered, Your Grace. I await your answer, Your Grace. I wish God's happiness and good health to Your Grace. Dated from our Sar(var), 28 June, 1610.

I love and serve Your Grace like a mother.

Erzsébet Báthory

This is the last letter that we have from Countess Báthory to Ferenc Batthyány. The tone is business-like, as always, but one senses now that the relationship was beginning to fray, as it was fraying with Count Thurzó, likely as a result of the rumors mounting against her.

According to most commentators and local historians, the Viennese mansion is located at 12 Augustinerstraße, directly across the street from the Augustinian monastery and cathedral. During the proceedings against Countess Báthory, witnesses alleged that she tortured girls here and that the screaming was so loud that the anguished monks nearby hurled their pots at the walls.

In the next letter written two months later in August, she again writes to Deputy Kisfaludi, this time asking him to follow up on the activities of two local troublemakers. She clearly expressing her weariness over the matter (or perhaps her situation in general):

Letter to Blazius Kysfaludi, August 27, 1610

May God grant goodness to both mind and body, Your Grace. Only by now ought Your Grace to have received our letter. Since then, we have been informed that there at the Raba (river), in the midst of the villages, at the edge of Chyavarga, Ist(van) Bokor and Deak Balas have gone from village to village. We would like to request, Your Grace, to bring us what news you hear, whether all there have shunned them at Chyavarga and all that might be if the saints of the village should support the pair, which things if yet doeth few things. Your Grace, many things we like on the one hand, yet grow weary from on the other. God grant you long life and good health. Dated from our Sárvár: 27 August, 1610.

G[enerose] E[gregia] D[omina] V[est]ra
In omnibus benevola (in all things wishing well)

Countess Erzsébet Báthory

THE FINAL DAYS: LETTERS AND DOCUMENTS FROM 1610 (INCLUDING EPILOGUE AND SUPPLEMENT)

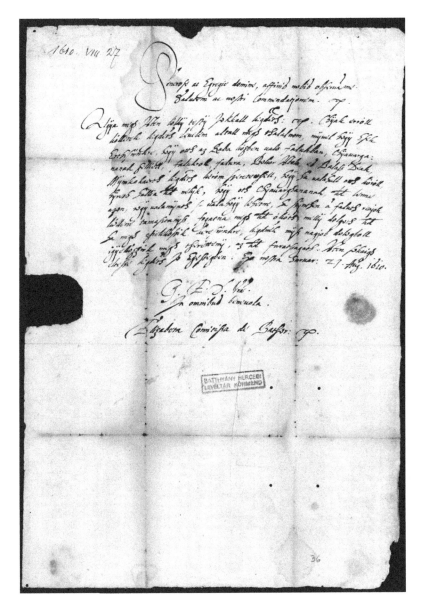

Letter to Blazius Kysfaludi, August 27, 1610

THE PRIVATE LETTERS OF COUNTESS ERZSÉBET BÁTHORY

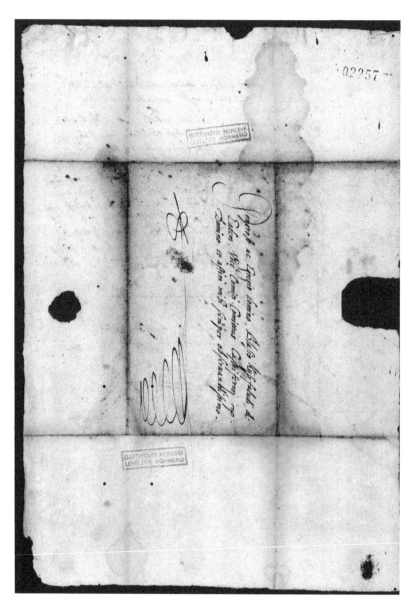

Backside/address, Letter to Kysfaludi, August 27, 1610

THE FINAL DAYS: LETTERS AND DOCUMENTS FROM 1610 (INCLUDING EPILOGUE AND SUPPLEMENT)

One month later, in September of that same year, Countess Báthory wrote her Last Will and Testament. In this document, she gave all of her property to her three children, Anna, Kata, and Pál, and requested only that she be allowed to keep her wedding dress for her lifetime. There is no mention here of her children András or Orsolya (Orsika), or Miklós, for that matter. We must assume that András and Orsolya are since deceased and, although Miklós lived long enough to marry a member of the Zrínyi family, that he was indeed not one of her children or, at least not one of her legitimate heirs (one does have to wonder, about the following, though: in 1615, Pál Nádasdy completed the fortification on Sárvár Castle begun by his father in 1588. Upon completion, Pál posted a plaque identifying himself as his father's "legitimate heir." It is unclear whether he wrote that out of convention or to make a point.)

LAST WILL AND TESTAMENT OF ERZSÉBET BÁTHORY, SEPTEMBER 3, 1610

I, noble and gracious Erzsébet Báthory, the widow of the former noble and gracious Ferenc Nádasdy, covered by God's grace, now in old age and without strength, in an ailing state, am obliged to tend to matters that cause me excruciating suffering due to the passing of my blessed and beloved husband, weakening me from day to day. Many restless concerns came over me as to my three beloved children, when my two unmarried daughters and my un-tutored son came into the care and custody of my widowed hands. Until now, I have supplied them, with God's gracious help, by assiduous care and motherly love, despite my widowed standing, not only for their good and their

THE PRIVATE LETTERS OF COUNTESS ERZSÉBET BÁTHORY

physical nourishment relating to their benefit; especially also, as the almighty God in His gracious goodness with my two daughters Anna and Kata Nádasdy therein showed luck, praised and blessed be His holy name, for all the orphans and widows to whom He graciously provides. I have provided decently for them at appropriate times, through their father's house, and their parents bore the appropriate costs of marriage—my older daughter Anna to the highly well-born and gracious Miklós Zrínyi, Kata to the most high-born and gracious György Homonnay, where I paid the expenses and took care of the major concerns. I cared, thanks to the gracious help of God, praised and blessed be His holy name, also for the education of my son Pál Nádasdy, such that he, as the almighty God declared the time to have come, at twelve years of age took the oath of office of County Chief at the county of Vas in a proper manner and with corresponding costs paid. And because for all these things I zealously bore these concerns, my awareness now dwindling, thanks to the strength and holy grace of God, from day to day without ceasing I am still able to think about the end of my earthly life with all my heart, and have decided that to the end of my life, I shall think only of the holy, gracious God, the Savior and Creator, and prove to Him my gratitude. For this reason, I renounce earthly concerns and clarify hereby by this Testament that I have renounced the care and possession of the father's portion for my children, including all of his movable and immovable goods, and, as of this day, wish to be carefree of worries about such desires, save for all the managers, assistants, and other faithful servants of my beloved husband's blessed memory who have been entrusted to me for their care and custody.

THE FINAL DAYS: LETTERS AND DOCUMENTS FROM 1610 (INCLUDING EPILOGUE AND SUPPLEMENT)

Since the father's portion has not yet been divided amongst my children, and while also my two daughters currently live distantly away with their husbands, since Pál Nádasdy my son lives with me, I have left him in possession of the goods, and he shall let it remain so until God allows my three children to come together and divide the goods with the help of their pious, God-fearing relatives and friends of the most important neighboring men with whom in loving kinship this agreement has been made.

Hereby, I have asked both my daughters and sons-in-law to wait for their brother to come of age before distributing the goods acquired from Sárvár, Kapuvár, and Leka and not to cause any harm to come to them. May they among one another find an equitable manner in which to share, such that the rights of a child living after the death of another child be not diminished. The remaining goods, both the father's portion as well as the mother's portion, that have come to be located everywhere in this country, no matter which county they are located, are to be divided in three portions. As for my bridal gown, which I shall wear until my death, what a reward it would be for me to allow my three children, from their share of goods, both to me, not as their mother, as well as other relatives to pay nothing; because I have them and because I have them naturally and also frequently equally permit, that they in the future never need to pay for the goods coming into their hands.

As far as inherited property and legacies that came to me by my father and my mother are concerned, everything I've previously owned, and everything in the future that would go to me after my due share of in-

THE PRIVATE LETTERS OF COUNTESS ERZSÉBET BÁTHORY

heritance and, whether by virtue of blood, whether by virtue of a Testament, blessed by my parents or brethren, as I could or would have had a claim—I have transferred all of this with full inheritance rights to my three children, Anna Nádasdy, Kata Nádasdy and Pál Nádasdy, and I also pass into their hands all my castles, together with their revenues. I also have included all of my property owned since childhood into their respective shares of ownership; I have also put into their hands all of the deeds, titles, and letters, as the decree so provides, and for which the law provides. The gold works, I have bequeathed to Pál Nádasdy because my two daughters have already received their shares; i.e., rings, hangers, etc. I have also bequeathed all my moveable goods, silver works, gems and however they may be called, to my three children in equal shares, except for the horse harness and weapons, since I had already bequeathed that to my son, Pál Nádasdy.

These are my orders and my Last Testament, shown by their own free will that I did call as witnesses certain important nobles, so that they could witness my orders and my Last Testament, from my mouth were words that were put in writing here, present together with me with their original seals and reaffirming their names as thus follows:

first: Bálint Récsey from Gátosháza
second: Kristóf Cicheo from Gulács
third: Márton Szopory from Fölsö-Szopor
fourth: István Döry from Jobaháza
fifth: István Tompa from Bódogfalva
sixth: János Bácsmegyei from Simaháza
seventh: Gergely Piterius, a preacher from Keresztúr

THE FINAL DAYS: LETTERS AND DOCUMENTS FROM 1610 (INCLUDING EPILOGUE AND SUPPLEMENT)

eighth: Benedek Deseö from Haraszt
ninth: Gergely Pásztori from Bozd
tenth: Vid Andy de And
eleventh: Miklós Madarász.

This testament is given at Keresztúr, 3 September, 1610.

Erzsébet Báthory

A comparison of signatures here is interesting:

Signature typically found on Batthyány letters.

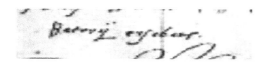

Signature found on the Will.

The handwriting in the will is most likely not hers, and the signature is unusual. Nowhere in the will do we see the beautiful penmanship found in her letters to Batthyány. The signature lacks the M.P. designator and has either been penned by a scribe or written by the Countess in a time of poor health. We do know that around this time, she headed to the spa at Piest'any, and the document itself references her ailing health.

THE PRIVATE LETTERS OF COUNTESS ERZSÉBET BÁTHORY

Around that same time, she returned briefly to Sárvár. The castle was undergoing a renovation, and it appears she knew then that she would not be spending the Christmas holidays there. She collected her jewels, baggage, and furnishings and assembled her retinue to proceed to Csejthe before the roads became impassable. Roads, in those days, were frequently blocked by snow during January and February, and winter travel was quite limited.

This author speculates the following: we know that in her Last Will and Testament, Countess Báthory divested herself of all of her property, giving it to her children and keeping only a life estate in her wedding gown. In November, she wrote to Gábor Báthory, asking for a document that likely named him, as well as another Báthory relative, to serve as executors or trustees of the estate on behalf of her children (see below). The Countess then collected her personal items and left for Csejthe, an estate which she owned outright, having received it as a wedding gift and redeemed it in full with the Crown some years prior. Perhaps she intended at the time—and as history would later determine—to spend the remainder of her days there. In any case, she arrived in October of 1610.

On October 20, 1610, Countess Báthory penned an angry letter to György Thurzó who, the previous year, had been raised to the office of Palatine. From the tone of the letter, it is clear that, by this time, their relationship had broken down. Countess Báthory was also likely aware now of Thurzó's legal machinations proceeding against her and, in his position of Chief Justice, he was clearly aware of the allegations against her.

The contents are paraphrased here: One of Thurzó's servants, Kaspar Pattai, went into the nearby market town of Vág Újhely with some of Countess Báthory's servants. Pattai became drunk and then, on the way home, got into a fight with one of these servants, challenging him to a duel. The fight was bro-

THE FINAL DAYS: LETTERS AND DOCUMENTS FROM 1610 (INCLUDING EPILOGUE AND SUPPLEMENT)

ken up, and the men parted company. However, Pattai then went to the home of the Countess' servant and deliberately cut the legs of his horse. After that, Pattai went to the Countess' manor home looking for the man again, cursing and challenging him to another duel. At this point, the servant came out; the two men engaged in a duel until the Countess' servant broke his sword and Pattai fled. Some time later, Pattai again returned to the manor, swearing and causing trouble. Countess Báthory informed Thurzó that this information could be corroborated by György Zalay and Michael Baranyai, servants of her son-in-law, Miklós Zrínyi, who was visiting her at the time with her daughter, Anna. The Countess then assured Thurzó that her own servant had done nothing to provoke this and would have been punished accordingly if he had. She then requested that Thurzó forbid Pattai from coming to her house any further and, in his office as palatine, to protect her from such abuse.

It is interesting to note that Countess Báthory only named the witnesses to the event but not the servant actually involved in the dispute with Pattai. It might have been her henchman, Ficzkó (János Ujváry), an adolescent who, as mentioned, was later executed as an accomplice in the murders of so many servant girls. Sárvár Judge, Gergely Páztory (one of the witnesses to Countess Báthory's Will) testified that his own servant had once been provoked into a fight by this brutal young man, that Ficzkó ran about the estates causing trouble, that he bragged about the murders, and that the Countess continuously protected him despite this. Judge Páztory testified that he himself once asked the Countess why she kept "such a bad man" at her court.

Not surprisingly, during this stressful period, more girls died. According to witnesses, during the Zrínyis' visit, the entire female staff was sent upstairs and ordered to remain there. Things got out of hand when Dorottya Szentes began starving and freezing the girls to keep them in order. At one point, Countess Báthory sent for one of the girls to accompany her and daughter Anna to the nearby spa at Piestány. It was soon reported that not a single girl was physically able to make the trip. Enraged, the Countess declared that Szentes should not have taken things so far. Nevertheless, witnesses reported that, after reviving the girls, Szentes and the Lady Báthory mercilessly beat them all to death.

Certainly knowing that she was running out of time, Countess Báthory continued to put her estate in order for the benefit of her children. Around that time, she requested a legal document from Gábor Báthory, which required two signatures: one from Gábor and, likely, the other from András Báthory (referenced only as "our brother"). Gábor Báthory wrote the following reply:

> *I received your letter in which you ask me and our good brother to send to you a Procurator (power of attorney). I shall send to you my part immediately, but our brother is not here now. I have sent for him and as soon as he is here he will send you his letter also. I had this document taken from the abbey and from our chancellery and sent to you. Only ask and we shall help you in whatever you wish, your loving family. May God grant you long life and good health. At your service with love. 6 November, 1610.*
>
> *Gábor Báthory*

The term *Procurator* refers to a proctor, or procuracy, which then, as now, is a proxy or power of attorney, in which one party agrees to represent the legal interests of another or receive their benefits, such as in the case of a trustee. This would make sense: Countess Báthory had just completed her Will. She would

THE FINAL DAYS: LETTERS AND DOCUMENTS FROM 1610 (INCLUDING EPILOGUE AND SUPPLEMENT)

have likely requested that her family members administer the property on her behalf or hold the estate in trust for her children, particularly on behalf of her minor son, Pál, as she had legally divested herself of the property. In addition, in those days, estate administration was under the domain of the clergy, and Count Báthory stated that the documents were taken from the abbey and chancellery, both under the domain of religious authority.

Benedek Deseö testified that by this time, Countess Báthory was receiving legal advice from advisors "on both sides of the Danube." He claimed that he and the other servants had begged her to stop what she doing and that she would be arrested. The Countess replied that she was above arrest. On the side, however, she was clearly divesting herself of her property so that it could pass safely to her children and avoid seizure in the coming criminal prosecution.

These are the last known correspondences of Countess Erzsébet Báthory. One month later, just after Christmas, György Thurzó and his men apprehended her and her servants after raiding her manor home at Csejthe.

THE PRIVATE LETTERS OF COUNTESS ERZSÉBET BÁTHORY

Count György Thurzó, Palatine of Hungary (1567-1616)

Count Thurzó lying in state.

THE FINAL DAYS: LETTERS AND DOCUMENTS FROM 1610 (INCLUDING EPILOGUE AND SUPPLEMENT)

EPILOGUE

We have very little in the way of private letters concerning Countess Báthory's summary trial and sentencing. Her son-in-law, Miklós Zrínyi, corresponded with Thurzó, and some of those letters have been preserved. Her son, Pál, also wrote to Thurzó on his mother's behalf, of which that correspondence remains. We also have one letter from Thurzó's wife, who simply wondered whether the allegations against Erzsébet Báthory were true (the reader can find all of these letters in *Infamous Lady: The True Story of Countess Erzsébet Báthory*). But, to date, there is no known correspondence from her friend Ferenc Batthyány, or Pál Nyáry, or her family members, including Prince Gábor Báthory—whom, after her incarceration, Countess Báthory firmly believed would rescue her.

The record, as it stands, seems to suggest that only a handful stood by her at the end. The rest were not willing to challenge the king on behalf of the Widow Nádasdy, or even lend support to her position. It is likewise interesting that of over 300 witnesses interrogated by the king's officials, no one from amongst Countess Báthory's family was called to speak. She herself was not permitted to testify, although she did give a statement to Thurzó asserting that any wrongdoing was solely the result of her servants' actions. Likewise, few of her friends and none of her family from amongst the high nobility were called to testify, even though the king's notaries were ordered to summon people of both low and high birth, and from amongst both the clergy and laity.

In the end, Countess Báthory died in captivity in August of 1614. Her cousin, Prince Gábor Báthory, never did rescue her. He died the year before her, having been murdered by two of his own officers. His rival, Gábor Bethlen, replaced him on the Transylvanian throne, installed there by the Habsburgs. György Thurzó died not long after, in 1616; his widow, Erzsébet Czobor, who famously stole Countess Báthory's jewelry during her imprisonment, herself became the victim of greedy relatives and died in poverty. King Mátyás, the Habsburg who strenuously sought Countess Báthory's punishment to the fullest extent of the law, died in 1619. Family friend, Ferenc Batthyány, was never called to testify and, to date, there is no evidence that he attempted to help Countess Báthory during her legal proceedings. He died on September 13, 1625.

SUPPLEMENT

TWO LETTERS OF FERENC NÁDASDY (1585)

It is unfortunate that so few writings of Ferenc Nádasdy remain to us—far fewer than even that of his wife. Two private letters are preserved in the Batthyány Archives, however, which provide a glimpse into the couple's life during the tenth year of their marriage in December of 1585. The two are spending time at Castle Csejthe, the estate that would someday become infamous as the site of so many murders and Countess Báthory's final imprisonment. Both letters are written to Count Miklós Pálffy, a military colleague of Ferenc Nádasdy.

THE FINAL DAYS: LETTERS AND DOCUMENTS FROM 1610 (INCLUDING EPILOGUE AND SUPPLEMENT)

Ferenc Nádasdy's Letter to Miklós Pálffy, December 3, 1585

That/may the Lord God grant that we can soon visit your beautiful baby boy. Truly, my heart sings with joy. May the Holy Lord grant you great happiness and joy and bless you with all good wishes, Amen. I understand from your letter that the Behrami troops/unit will provide the Pasha and also a good horse, and that the good news will be spread by your servants and not delayed. Also, that you kindly command accordingly next week to go to you. And God (it give is worth....things thou...) God grant you good health and long life, Your Grace, both your wife and you and your beautiful son forever. From Csejthe, 3 December, 1585.

S(ervi)tor et Fr(ater) Addictiss(imus).

Fran(ciscus) Nadasdy, Manu p(ro)p(ria)

The baby referenced in this letter is István II, born at Pozsony and named after his uncle, István I. The baby would later grow up to become the Count of Pozsony County. Miklós Pálffy also had another child around this time, named Mark, born in 1584 and deceased by 1586.

In the next letter, we learn that the young couple is spending the Christmas Holidays at Castle Csejthe. Countess Báthory must have been quite ill at the time. Her husband writes to Count Pálffy that, as a result of this illness, he cannot come in person to discuss a business matter regarding a fellow lord. Count Nádasdy also declines an upcoming holiday invitation in

THE PRIVATE LETTERS OF COUNTESS ERZSÉBET BÁTHORY

order to stay with his wife, which suggests that he intended to remain by her side for some time:

Ferenc Nádasdy to Miklós Pálffy, Dec. 21, 1585

I yet arrived this evening. As God provides my health, I still need to speak with you regarding what I have done/carried out with Lord Dobo (likely Ferenc Dobo). Immediately, I went to go to Your Grace, but my wife was found/discovered sick. I think, nevertheless, that by the Lord God there is no holiday to be had for me, and that I cannot go to the feast. Rather, God will provide my health, this Christmas, and shall intervene, Your Grace. That is also the day when I can write to Your Grace, only to request, at your service, that we can meet up/reach nearby. I still apologize for this, but I reassure Your Grace of my good wishes and that I am at your service. May the Lord God grant Your Grace long life and good health, and all of yours. From Csejthe, 21 December, 1585.

S(ervi)tor et Fr(ater) Addictiss(imus).

Fran(ciscus) Nadasdy, Manu p(ro)p(ria)

THE FINAL DAYS: LETTERS AND DOCUMENTS FROM 1610 (INCLUDING EPILOGUE AND SUPPLEMENT)

Count Ferenc Nádasdy (1555-1604)

THE PRIVATE LETTERS OF COUNTESS ERZSÉBET BÁTHORY

Count Miklós Pálffy (1552-1600)

APPENDIX

ORIGINAL SOURCE MATERIAL

E 185 Nádasdy Archives, Magyar Országos Levéltár (Hungarian National Archives), Budapest.

> Includes letters written by Erzsébet Báthory, addressed to: György Bánffy, Benedek Deseö, the Egervary Potencia, András Hájas, Ferenc Nádasdy, Pál Nyáry, István Szuhay, György Thurzó, and András Thar. 23 letters are addressed to Imre Vasváry.

P 1314 Batthyány Missiles/Letters of Erzsébet Báthory, Magyar Országos Levéltár, Budapest.

> Letters P 1314, numbered 02236-02252, and 02256, are addressed to Ferenc Batthyány (17 in total); numbers 02253-02255, and 02257, are addressed to Blazius Kisfaludi (4 in total).

Testament of Erzsébet Báthory, September 3, 1610. Fascicle E 142, Act. publ. fasc. 44 no. 25, Magyar Országos Levéltár, Budapest.

The Slovak National Archives, Bratislava, Palffy, AIL 3rd FASC. VII, fol. 13-14.

The State Regional Archives in Bytca (Státny oblastny Bytca archiv (SOBA), Fascicle OK, Thurzo correspondence, sign. II.

Werböczy, István, *Opus Tripartitum Juris Consuetudinarii Hungariae, 1514.*

BIBLIOGRAPHY

Bálint, Ila, *A Thurzó-család levéltára*, Királyi Magyar Egyetemi Nyomda, Budapest, 1932.

Báró, Béla Radvánszky, *Magyar családélet és háztartás a XVI. És XVII. Században*, vol. 3, Budapest, 1879.

Burke, P. (editor), *Economy and Society in Early Modern Europe*, RKP, London (1972).

Craft, Kimberly L., *Infamous Lady: The True Story of Countess Erzsébet Báthory*, CreateSpace, 2009.

Erdély Múzeum-Egyesület Akadémiai Kiadó, Kolozsvár, Budapest, 1997.

Radvánszky Báró, Béla, Magyar családélet és háztartás a xvi. és xvii. században, vol. 3, Budapest, 1879.

Szábo, T. Attila, et al., *Erdélyi Magyar Szótörténti Tár, I-VII*, Bucharest-Budapest, 1975-1995.

Thorne, Tony, *Countess Dracula: The Life and Times of the Blood Countess, Elisabeth Báthory*, Bloomsbury, 1998

Várkonyi, Gábor, *New Resources on the Life of Erzsébet Báthory*, Journal of Literature Communications, 103rd, vol. 1-2, pp. 181-204, 1999.

Wigand, C.F., *Presburg und seine Umgebung*, Presburg, 1865.

ELECTRONIC REFERENCES

Botos, László, The Homeland Reclaimed, Part Two, Hungary Under Foreign Occupation, Institute of Hungarian Studies http://www.magtudin.org/Homeland%20-%20Part%202.htm

Turner, Francis, Money and Exchange Rates in 1632, projects.exeter.ac.uk/RDavies/arian/current/howmuch.html (includes a database on old money, including currency, measure and weight conversion)

http://www.hs-deutschkreutz.at/lehmden/lehmden_schloss_e.html (history of Keresztúr)

http://www.batthyany.at/17_jahrhundert.html?&L=1 (History of the Batthyány family)

(http://www.nemzetijelkepek.hu/onkormanyzat-kormend_en.shtml) (History of the Batthyány family and Castle Körmend)

http://www.zo-fi.hu/tataipatara/?p=6 (Count Miklós Pálffy)

http://www.oenb.at/en/welcome_to_the_oenb.jsp (Economic history of Central Europe, from the Austrian National Bank)

For more information on Countess Erzsébet Báthory, you may enjoy the definitive English biography by the same author: *Infamous Lady: The True Story of Countess Erzsébet Báthory*. Available at Amazon.com.

Paperback: 340 pages
Publisher: CreateSpace (2009)
Language: English
ISBN-10: 1449513441
ISBN-13: 978-1449513443

For those wishing to correspond with the author and to share research, questions, or comments, please visit the website at www.InfamousLady.com. You are invited to join with Kimberly Craft and other Báthory scholars and enthusiasts at the Community of Báthory Scholars & Enthusiasts. Membership is free (www.InfamousLady.com). Find us on Facebook, too!

Made in the USA
Columbia, SC
08 July 2023